THE DOG IT WAS THAT DIED

Alan Coren's contributions to *Punch* and
the *Evening Standard*, his bestselling
IDI AMIN books and his many humour
collections, including the recent highly
successful GOLFING FOR CATS and THE
SANITY INSPECTOR, have established him
as one of the funniest writers in Britain today.
Coren fans have been eagerly awaiting
the reissue of this, his first book, published
in the mid-Sixties when the Satire Boom
was at its crescendo. Reviewers then were
unanimous in hailing Alan Coren's brilliant
comic observation.

'A comic genius' *The Times*

'Constantly funny, constantly true'
Evening Standard

'Alan Coren's satirical pieces are the real
thing: fresh, sharp and coloured with a
personal fantasy' *Daily Telegraph*

'A very topical comedian ... unusually
versatile' *Observer*

'One of our most consistent and prolific
funny writers' *Yorkshire Post*

**Also by the same author,
and available in Coronet Books:**

All Except The Bastard
The Sanity Inspector
Golfing For Cats

The Dog It Was That Died

Alan Coren

CORONET BOOKS
Hodder and Stoughton

FOR ANNE

© 1965, 1976 Alan Coren

First published in Great Britain 1976
by Robson Books Ltd.

The author would like to thank the proprietors and
editors of *Punch*, *The Listener* and *The Atlantic Monthly*
for permission to reproduce material in this book.

Coronet edition 1978

Printed and bound in Great Britain for
Hodder and Stoughton Paperbacks, a
division of Hodder and Stoughton Ltd.,
Mill Road, Dunton Green, Sevenoaks,
Kent (Editorial Office: 47 Bedford
Square, London, WC1 3DP) by
Hunt Barnard Printing Ltd.,
Aylesbury, Bucks.

ISBN 0 340 22299 9

Contents

ME

Note

The southern desert of New Mexico is bisected by a single ribbon of white asphalt. It runs for a hundred miles, without a curve, without a hill, and without a town. There is nothing but the brick-red sand, the cobalt sky, and the white road. And one thing more. Roughly halfway along this strip stands a hoarding, some fifty feet square, on thin black stilts. On it are the words: MENTAL HEALTH IS YOUR CONCERN. Nothing else.

In the three years since I saw it, I have never written about this sign. Thought about it, yes; but only very briefly, because of a nagging fear that if I think about it just that tiny bit too much, I shall start shrieking, or go bald. That hoarding is the testament of the new Ozymandias. I hope only that the imminent cataclysm will leave it intact, so that some intergalactic Shelley picking among Earth's rubble for buried metaphors may light upon it and knock up a cautionary tale for the androids back home.

I tell the story now for no other reason than that the publishers tell me I have a responsibility to my readers to give them some idea of what they're in for from this page on. The idea of responsibility so paralysed me that the only movement I could make was to pass the buck. I hope the copywriters for the New Mexico Health Department find it in their hearts to forgive me.   A. C.

 US

Dry Krapp

On the morning of June 28th, can there have been a *Sunday Times* reader among you who did not suddenly lurch in his bed scattering toastcrusts and E.P.N.S. willy-nilly and spilling the Maxwell House across his wife's *Express* with one single gust of David Tomlinson upstagery? Breathes there a man with soul so dead, he did not hurl back the bedclothes, do his side-splitting Groucho Marx walk several times around the room, and, pausing only to drop a couple of oranges into a handy bra and strap them to his chest, belt out the denouement of *Charley's Aunt*? Because, if such a man exists, he has forfeited forever the right to call himself a theatre-lover.

As for me, I was half-way through a soulful soft-shoe routine atop the wardrobe when my wife, a stonehearted girl from whom the decline and fall of the Holborn Empire could elicit no more than a curt yawn, wrenched my ukelele from me and asked what the hell I was playing at.

'Listen to this!' I cried, snatching off a one-piece nose and humorous ears outfit I managed to pick up for a song when Collins's Music Hall folded, 'Kenneth Pearson sights a new trend! Farce, he says, is back in. The West End is to be taken by storm. The Whitehall is opening with a riotous new funfeast entitled – oh, joy! – *Chase Me Comrade*. And in the autumn Rix is producing – wait for it – *The Diplomatic Baggage*. Nor is this all. Michael Codron is reviving *See How They Run* – God, how I split my sides over that in 1945 – and *Rookery Nook*. And Peter Hall, OUR OWN PETER HALL, darling, is considering *Thark!*'

9

'*Thark?*'

'Yes! *Thark*, that *schweinerei fantasque* of 1927, that quintessence of everything that the name Ben Travers implies.'

Obviously unable to cope with the ecstatic trauma that at that moment must have been cutting her to the very quick, she fell asleep. I, for my part, raced into the bathroom, slipped three or four times on the soap, executed a couple of fast pratfalls for good measure, and, changing into a red flannel nightshirt I had been keeping for just such an occasion, hid in the laundry basket.

I was shaken out of my impression of Robertson Hare (no small accomplishment, crouched as I was beneath a bouilla-baisse of alien socks) by that exquisite Aldwych *deus ex machina*, the doorbell. I leapt from cover, corked a moustache on my face, and, stopping only to hide under the spare bed and call 'Oo eez eet?' in faultless *au pair*, I opened the door. It was either my wife's first husband (left for dead at Fort Zinderneuf) or my own current mistress, disguised as the milkman.

'I say, I say, I say!' I said.

He stared at me with the endearing cunning of an idiot.

'Two pound fourteen and eight, eggs included,' he muttered.

'Clive!' I shouted, 'you've come back. Or is it Mummy?'

He thrust the bill into my hand, and slammed the door. I did a quick double-take at the bill, clapped a hand to my brow, and fainted. As the bedroom door opened on cue, my eyelids fluttered.

'The swine got away with the priceless green eye of the little yellow God, given us at our wedding by your only surviving relative, rich, eccentric Uncle Barnaby, who is visiting us today for the first time in twenty years to see the gem before he dies and leaves us the money to save Rotgut Towers from falling into the hands of the Chinese trans-vestite who has such a peculiar hold over our adopted daughter Mabel,' I whispered.

Shooting me a glance of that ambiguous tenderness mis-interpretable only by those kitchen cynics who cannot understand the unshakeable rock on which modern marriage is founded, she took a suitcase from the hall-cupboard and began to pack.

She'll come back, of course. It was simply that the shock of fulfilment requires an iron nerve. For longer than I care to remember, we two have been awaiting the return of English theatre to its rightful heritage. We are just about the smartest cookies in the theatre-set; we have deliberately avoided more Pinter first-nights than anyone in the trade, we saw the whole of *Beyond the Fringe* in Oxford cabaret, we know that *The World of Paul Slickey* was the greatest thing Osborne ever wrote, and we said that Tynan was over the hill just when everyone else was saying how young he was to pull down an *Observer* job. We have the largest collection of unproduced German expressionist drama in the neighbourhood, we never fail to catch the underlying symbolism of the Royal Tournament, we always laugh uproariously at the bits they never translate in the Noh plays and explain what was left out to our friends four rows in front, and, at the end of a Stratford season, we never fail to point out that we would gladly give up the whole of *Lear* if only we could keep those exquisite bits of business in *Two Gentlemen*. And, of course, we're infallible on the question of farce. Farce, along with bullfighting and druidical moots, is the only pure theatre. Farce is the only permissible refinement of mime, wherein we recognise man's primeval mimetic impulse, uncluttered by verbiage, unshackled to meretricious intellect. Years before the smart reviewers cottoned on to the idea, we had recognised that a Crazy Gang audience, when it thought it was merely laughing at dirty jokes, was really taking part in a group-ritual as old as cliché itself. And, naturally, the highlight of our theatre-going year is Bertram Mills's Circus.

When, as a small boy, I first became aware of the fundamental non-choice facing existential man, I immediately saw that the non-answer could only be non-resolved by farce. I like to think of myself as the creator of absurd drama, but I wouldn't push it. I would have banged out a couple of sizzling soupçons of anti-drama myself, were it not that ceasing to be an anti-writer would impugn my integrity, and when people began to rave over Ionesco and Pinter, a carefully cupped hand shielded them from the superiority of my smile. I was happy that the quasi-intellectuals were actually *enjoying* drama after all these years, and finding a justification, what's more, for having a

11

giggle at the knockabout act of *Godot*. And now that Rix, Travers, and their ilk are bound to become the darlings of with-it audiences from Chichester to Oberammergau, I am content merely that the convictions of a decade are their own vindication.

The only thing that still bothers me, now that we're on the threshold of a new Elizabethan age in drama, is how the boys who've sweated to bring it about are going to shape up. Has Pinter, say, after years of having to inject chunks of serious theme into his farces to get them past cagey critics, spoiled himself for his true vocation of *farceur*? Will Sam Beckett be able to recall that all the confusion about who Podso and Godot represent was all due to the fact that his pantomime didn't quite come off?

At a guess, I'd say we're in for a dicey transitional period on the boards. 1965 will probably see a plethora of plays with titles like 'Waiting for Chips with Charley's Aunt', until the boys find their feet. We'll have sets by Sean Kenny, consisting of great revolving chamber-pots and art-nouveau bathing-machines, and dustbins down-stage left under the rhinestone chandeliers. There'll be musique concrete on hand-wound gramophones, while tramps serve daiquiris to one another and decolleté maids chase in and out of bedrooms squealing stuff about the class-struggle and the decline of the West. In the dustbins, Jewel, Warriss, and Peter O'Toole will be singing 'One of the Ruins that Cromwell Knocked About a Bit', and in the orchard beyond the French windows, Kenneth Connor will be decapitating Hugh Griffith three times a night, while the Beatles sing Mahler in the pit.

Eventually, of course, it'll all settle down, and 1966 or 7 should see Jimmy Wheeler and Denholm Elliott (The Chocolate Coloured Coon) firmly entrenched at the Court, belting out the pristine folk-art and swotting one another with custard pies for the titillation of the masses. They will naturally be laughing their guts out and missing the whole point; but at least it'll give us intellectuals something to get our teeth into.

Value for Money

'The Royal Philatelic Society is to sell part of the unique collection of early Italian stamps bequeathed to it in 1914 by Prince Alphonse Doria Pamphilj, then one of the best-known philatelists in the world. The most valuable item is a Sicilian half-grano printed in error in blue instead of in yellow. It is one of two recorded examples and is expected to fetch over £5,000. Both copies were originally on one letter found by a boy in Syracuse, Sicily, about 1890. One stamp was removed and the one left on the envelope went into the Ferrari collection which was sold in the 1920's by the French Government as part of German war reparations. The present owner is unknown.'

The Daily Telegraph

I ought to make it quite clear that I'm not one of those men who nudges you in the Tube to point out that the price paid to keep a Leonardo in the country is equivalent to 743 council houses. Nor have I ever dared assess the value of a book to anyone but myself: is fifteen bob (= 1 set of cellular underwear) too low a price for a Collected Shakespeare? Would £65 (= 1 telly) be nearer the mark? What's it worth to hear the Eroica? Similarly, if a bloke runs up to pluck my sleeve and tell me he's just bumped into a woman who's price is above rubies, I won't offer him an argument. Without, perhaps, fully appreciating the worth such things represent, I'm capable of recognising the reasons for it.

Not with stamps, though. Their value is never established in terms I understand. Those enormous pre-Raphaelite jobs

13

that flow incessantly from Central European presses, depicting in minute Technicolor detail the siege of Stalingrad or the Hungarian football team, turn up in job-lots in the *Boy's Own Paper* at two bob a thousand, while a misprinted scrap picked out of the gutter by a Sicilian beggar on a dog-end hunt gets knocked down in Bond Street for £5,000. Oh, I know about rarity value; it's the basis of that very propensity that bothers me. I can think of nothing else that comes under the gavel simply because it happens to be an inferior specimen of its breed. A diamond doesn't soar in value because it's chipped and turns grey in the rain. An inferior Rembrandt fetches less than a masterpiece. Bidders don't engage in punch-ups in the aisles because a Sévres milkmaid with three ears has finally come up for auction. Stamps, however, depend for their worth on the pure accident of somebody's ineptitude. A chap stops his serrating machine to put the kettle on, and the result is a row of stamps with holes in the middle to render them priceless. Sometimes the rarity is caused by a miserable disaster; perhaps it involved the brave lads working after hours to turn out the first day's issue of the Borneo 2c green when a party of locals surrounded the tent, ate the printer and his mates, and burned everything in sight except for a block of 2c green, picked out of the rubble years later by a Stanley Gibbons safari.

One wonders whether these gems are really worth saving. On that day when the curators of our culture are glancing in terror at the skies and stuffing a hurried selection of treasures into bomb-proof hampers for the benefit of posterity, will they make room for a blue half-grano from Sicily with a note to the effect that because it wasn't yellow it was worth two reasonable Picassos? How will our heirs react when they dig up the Mona Lisa to discover she has one eye on either side of her nose and no moustache, yet still seemed to retain some value for their peculiar ancestors?

Perhaps I ought to have met a philatelist or two, or strolled among the revellers at some Stampmen's Annual Funfeast, joking about swops and tweezers. As it is, I imagine them as a race of desperate unshaven men with bi-focals and nervous hands, living in great brown Victorian houses in Streatham and Penge cluttered up with yellowing loose-leaf folders and dusty glass cases; men who sleep on camp-beds

14

in the hall, who wake two minutes before the postman comes and leap horribly upon the mail with steaming kettles and magnifying-glasses, rabid for an odd shade of magenta or an inverted head. Or perhaps they're all like Prince Alphonse Doria Pamphilj, relics of the Golden Age of Philately, fat, tired moguls surrounded by their tatty treasures, propped up in a tasselled bed with a telephone in each hand, in hourly contact with their stampbrokers, shouting: 'BUY!' 'SELL!' 'HOLD!' and sending parties of asthmatic clerks through the stamp collections of the dead, searching, searching, searching. Really, one can't but think of such characters as a pretty distasteful bunch; what other joys but those of greed and exclusive possession are to be won from sitting in Harmer's salerooms, bidding in thousands, and carting off the exorbitant prize for a long winter's gloat?

Nevertheless, I'd been prepared to allow each man his own eccentricity until I saw that bit about the *other* Sicilian half-grano having been sold by the French as part of German war reparations. There's an element of black farce about the involvement of this Sicilian misprint in the wretched machinery of war, and death-compensation, a sense of out-of-jointedness. What did the half-grano fetch in 1920? Four dead officers? Sixteen enlisted men? We may never find out now; the present owner is unknown. One hopes he's happy with his possession, that's all.

Still, I have to admit that a fair part of my own bitterness is concerned with the agglomeration of misshapen junk I have accumulated at enormous irretrievable expense over the years. These *objets grotesques* have never quite made the saleroom grade, and I fail to see why. After all, they're unique, with the exact credentials that qualify the half-grano as a prestigious collector's item. I have, for instance, a navy-blue jacket (originally part of a set, the blue trousers having been snapped up in a jumble sale, present owner unknown) which was supposed to have been made in grey, but due to oversight and incompetence, wasn't. In addition to this priceless blunder, the item also has one sleeve longer than the other, and is shy of a breast pocket. There's no other like it in existence, I swear. I have, too, a clock which runs backwards and chimes every twelve minutes, a treasure that has deceived horologists throughout the civilised world. And, in unwrapping it just the other day, I spotted that the

1951 *Manchester Guardian* in which it was swaddled contains the word 'skinch', a palpable misprint that to my knowledge has not reappeared. Now, there can't be more than – what? – fifty copies of this particular paper still in mint condition, and most of those will be in sacrosanct files. And this is no mere shrivelled-up square inch of mouldy paper; the lucky buyer would have a full square yard of densely packed misprints for his money, which, at half-grano rate, ought to put it in the million-pound bracket.

But I don't intend to let it stop there. It so happens that the Albanian government, adjudged guilty by the International Court at the Hague in 1949 of sinking two British warships, still hasn't forked out the requisite £843,947. Let's not be too harsh on them; maybe it's not easy for the Albanians to lay their hands on ready money. But for the sake of easing Anglo-Albanian relations, I am prepared to offer my entire collection to them to be sold at whatever auctioneer's they choose. It can't be worth less than two million, but I'm no philatelic shark; I'm prepared to let the lot go for a hundred thousand. Honest.

Agents of the Last Estate

We had a filthy journey to Hampstead-on-the-Wold. I'm dead against taking Family Units house-hunting, but my wife insisted we needed them for measurement, so we dragged them along. They're always sick on the monorail; at least, the youngest F.U.3 and F.U.4 (Female) are – F.U.1 spends all his free time swotting, thank heavens, and F.U.2 is still on his craze of collecting mechanical-cow numbers; kneels for hours on end with his face pressed against the observation dome, muttering numerals into his dictaphone. I can't think on monos, myself; usually just watch the telly, or sleep.

Twenty minutes out of Central Hampstead the females threw up in unison, but by the time we'd gone through Outer Hampstead and Hampstead-on-the-Hill they'd perked up a bit, so the wife went back to chuckling over the micro-film gossip columns and I chewed on the odd nicotine tablet and listened to the Moon; not unpleasant. Then, just after Hampstead-on-Thames, F.U.1 had a fit in the middle of his History homework. Lately, I've been a bit worried about him – he tries, and he's managed to stay in the eighty-third stream at the Comprehensive, but it doesn't look as though he'll get into Rockall University after all; he's failed Applied Mnemonics twice, and he'll be nine next Ratesday, so there's little hope. He'll have to leave school, I suppose, and get used to leisure; it comes to all of us soon enough.

I managed to calm his sobs, and he settled.

'Come on, One, old chap,' I said. 'What's the trouble?'

'I'm so rotten at dates,' he muttered wetly. 'When did the Conversionists come to power?'

' '78,' I said. 'Didn't they teach you all the background stuff?'

He shook his head, and chewed his microphone wretchedly. I sat back.

'Well – in 1967,' I said, 'the West-Wing Democrats got in by a landslide on their Fair Housing campaign. But the whole thing was a fraud. Their adcopy had been written by Estatesmen P.R.s, of course, so the electorate didn't stand a chance. By the time they realised whom they'd *actually* voted for, the House of Commons, as it was called, was filled with 630 estate agents. First act they passed was the Acquisition of Parliamentary Freehold Act, which gave them statutory right to the House and choice of tenancy. We still had a second chamber then (called, after 1967, the House of Freeholders) which hurriedly forced through the Privy Reconstruction of Society Act, stratifying the population into Freeholders, Leaseholders, Tenants, Subtenants, and Bedsitters. Surely you've heard of the Bedsitters' Revolt?'

'1975,' said F.U.1 brightly. 'The Bedsitters March up Maida Vale, and the Storming of the Barricades at Notting Hill. Forcibly put down.'

'Jolly good,' I said. 'Of course, that was before the Regional Nomenclatures Act split Ancient London into Hampstead, to the north, and Mayfair, to the south. Do you realise, One, that once upon a time, in the sixties or so, there were places called Belsize Park and Chalk Farm and Golders Green and Swiss Cottage? Even before they got in, the Estatesmen were calling them Hampstead, but their Act made it official. My father remembers when Mayfair Station was called Victoria; and even Mayfair itself's disappeared now.'

'I know,' said One. He drew a breath. 'Greater Hampstead, population 37,000,000, is the biggest city in the world. It extends from the Wash to Littlehampstead-on-Sea.' He frowned. '*When* did the Conversionists get in?'

'1978. The West-Wing Democrats (they were for lateral expansion) were run out of office by the Conversionist Opposition (they were for vertical subdivision) and a splinter group called the Subterranean Deviationists. The coup mightn't have held without their leader, whose name escapes me; he was a German immigrant, and his campaign slogan: "LEBENSRAUM!" swept the country. Naturally, he never explained it, and after the coup he turned out to be not a revolutionary at all, but a diehard Conversionist.'

'I remember,' interrupted One. 'The Period of National Snuggery.'

'Right. He dropped ceilings four feet to give five floors instead of three, converted cupboards into Kosy Kiddie-rooms, developed the lavatory/dinette, and pushed through a private bill officially changing the name "Window-box" to "Minigarden". But he's best remembered for the inflatable tenement, and for his splendid work after the Great Communications Collapse.' I paused, and in the mono-railer's sigh, I seemed to catch the echo of a long-dead two-stroke. 'You won't remember roads, One; they used to connect different parts of Hampstead with one another, but since no money was spent on their upkeep, especially after all the roadmenders were put on full-time converting, they just withered away. One day, everything jammed.'

'Jammed?'

'Sorry, I forgot. In 1981, there were 58,000,000 cars on the island: metal boxes with little engines that kept them down to the regulation speed of four miles per hour – you must have seen pictures. Anyhow, one day there was no more space for them, and no carhouses, because these had all been converted into four-family snuggeries. So they all stopped where they were, and grass grew up around them, and pretty yellow weeds. Then one day, the Prime Estates-man looked out of his office window over Westminster Bridge; it was peculiarly quiet, and he turned to his body-guard and said: "Mein Gott, the very houses seem asleep," whereupon the bodyguard replied: "Them ain't 'ouses, them's cars." The P.E. paused for a moment, and murmured: "Earth haf not anything to show more fair." Within six weeks, all the cars in Greater Hampstead had been converted into bijou residences. Charming, actually; Mummy and I bought one – central heating, radio, picture windows, flushfitting doors, concealed lighting, two armchairs and a sofa. Awfully snug – wasn't it, dear?'

She looked up from the microfilm, smiled palely.

'Don't fill his head with marzipan,' she said. 'One family

to a whole car, indeed! He'll want his own hammock next.'

The monorailer slid to a halt. It was dusk now, but luckily there was an early moon. The corporation hover-craft hummed us over the rutted fields, past the slag-heaps and the rocket-range, and deposited us outside the electrified fence. We identified ourselves, and were quickly measured. For the first time, it seemed, I noticed how short F.U.1 was, and how bent. I'm four-feet-eleven, and the wife isn't small either; but F.U.1 isn't two feet tall yet. The Alsatians quite dwarfed him. Times change, I suppose.

Beyond the fence, the estate lay silent, a vast concrete meadow faintly phosphorescent beneath the rising moon. Some residences had already gone up, and dotted the luminous landscape, casting bizarre blue shadows. They were shaped like organ-pipes, groups of four, five, six tubes of differing heights.

'Clean,' said the Agent. 'Unfussy-styling. Space-saving.'

He led us to a plot marked off into an oblong of about twenty square feet. Beside it lay a length of cylindrical con-crete, stamped: H.U.D.C. Water Board. The Agent glanced at it, at us, and down at his notebook.

'I see there's fifteen-feet-seven-inches of you,' he said. He ran a measuring-tape along the tube. 'Twenty-one feet. Plenty. Allows for F.U. growth at plus-standard rate.' He blew a whistle, somewhere, a bloodhound bayed. After a minute or two a small machine trundled up, cut the tube into varying lengths, and rumbled back into the gathering darkness. A gang of converters manhandled the tubes up-right, in descending order.

'You'll need roofs, naturally,' said the Agent. 'And slumberhooks and foodpipes and tellypoints. But try them for comfort.'

The converters dropped our F.U.s into their compart-ments; I gave the wife a leg-up into hers, and climbed into my own. It was certainly cosy; touching the walls with my shoulders gave me a feeling of security, of possession.

'What do you think, dear?' I shouted.

An errie, half-human boom answered me. I couldn't dis-tinguish the words, so I hoisted myself to the top of my room and peered down into hers.

'I like it,' she said. 'It's compact.'

'Snug,' I said.

'Bijou,' said the Agent.

I dropped to the ground. 'How much are you asking?'

'I can offer you an eight-week lease at seventy per, nineteen hundred for f and f, rates a hundred a month. You're responsible for maintenance, drainage, H.E.P. upkeep, decomposition hazard, and Acts of God.'

'Sounds reasonable,' I said.

'It's a bargain,' shouted my wife from her slot. The echoes ran off into the darkness.

'*Reasonable?*' said the agent heavily. '*A bargain?*' He folded my cheque into his hatband, and nodded towards the line of tubes. 'It's the last word in living.'

The Islington Trend

I was lolling against an alabaster bust of Cecil Beaton, pondering a new colour scheme for my Olivetti and fingering my favourite conversation-piece, a Shirley Conran radish-grater, when the editor of the Colour Supplement burst in. He was not alone. Hanging to one impeccable mohair sleeve was our features editor, a small, bald man currently engaged in an article on the history of colour supplements (made up mainly of photographs of our photographers taking photographs of the painting in the Imperial War Museum), and the editor of our Industrial Supplement (at present running a series on the economics of publishing industrial supplements) with his brother-in-law, our cheese correspondent, and Eric, their tame potto.

'Good morning, Gentlemen!' I cried.

The editor scowled.

'Cut that!' he snapped. 'When I want comedy routines, I'll ask for them.' He whipped a Polaroid Land Camera from his shoulder-holster, took a couple of profiles of me, and peered at the finished prints.

'I thought so,' he muttered. 'You're my art editor, aren't you?'

'To the life,' I said, lowering my eyes softly. 'The eternally grateful man you saved from that Greek Street sweatshop and the endless drudgery of touching up postcards of au pair maids in handcuffs for the genuine collector. You'll never regret it, sir.'

'No?' he sneered, 'and what are you working on now?'

I pointed to the gilt Victorian hip-bath in which I keep my supply of half-tone blocks.

'A magnificent sixteen-page sepia-toned reconstruction entitled *Baroque Typography and its Influence on the War of Jenkin's Ear*,' I said. 'It's all there, sir, the joy, the tears, the Letraset, the . . . '

'TRASH!' he screamed. 'Is that the sort of stuff our advertisers want to read? What's happened to the crusading, lucrative spirit of 1964? Where is the trend-setting follow-up to our matchless features on teenage hair, our thirty pages on shirt-collar art, our magnificent colour-work of kinky boots reflected in Lambretta mudguards, our Hampstead Heath collages? Where is our social commitment, our sense of photogenic irony, our cosmic approach to the burning Bank Holiday issues? Where are our *trends*?'

'Oh, sir!' I cried, 'life has suddenly become so disparate, so unrelated! We've tried everything. We have forty men working on the possible tie-up between the Verrazzano Narrows Bridge, and the new Forth Bridge as a social phenomenon linking – not to say, bridging, ha-ha-ha – two continents, two, so to speak, ways of life, but it won't gell sociologically . . . '

The editor's face became an icy mask. I pulled out my Leica and snapped it for a series I plan to do some day on *Icy Masks of the Western Hemisphere*, but he tore the camera from my hand.

'What about Islington, you fool?'

The long silence was marred only by the scratching of the features editor's pen, and the potto's singing.

'Islington?' I said, at last.

'There have been six shootings there in a *week*!' shouted the editor. 'If that's not a trend, I'd like to know what is! By God, man, one more shooting, and it'll be a phenomenon. Don't you realise the significance of what I'm saying? Every other supplement in the business'll be down there by now, portraying, depicting, linking, relating, concluding . . . ' He opened the door. 'You have twenty-four hours.'

Within ten minutes, I and seven hand-picked members from the social commentators' pool were crouched in the Supplement's charabanc, bound for the Balls Pond Road. My heart pounded; the whole area teemed with possibility, with Cypriot children, Nigerians in their flowing robes contrasting so originally with the dullness of Victorian brick, with Italians in black shawls (the stark shapes, the pungent colouring!), with Irish labourers (those bucolic faces, out of place, out of time, in this bleak urban context!), with elderly bearded Jews (ah, ancient mystery!) – the 35-millimetre cassettes fell about my feet in an endless cascade. Islington seemed – to borrow a phrase, simultaneously coined by five of our writers – a very melting-pot of civilisation!

We pulled up outside a pockmarked pub, and, pausing only to snap an E-type Jag parked ironically outside a festering slum, we went inside. There were signs that rival gangs of social critics had beaten us to it; lens-caps, typewriter-ribbon, pencil stubs lay in the sawdust, and the reek of angostura thickened the air. The landlord was standing behind the bar, wearing his Eighth Army uniform and Arsenal rosette, with a wilting Michaelmas daisy in his mouth.

'Cheese!' he said, as I approached him. I wound on my film and, he gave me his card.

'Good morning,' I said, 'I'm investigating the sudden and terrifying outbreaks of . . . '

'Yes,' said the landlord. He cleared his throat. 'Yes, I would say there is a connection between all these incidents what have taken place in the environs of my hostelry, The Rat and Cockle in Mafeking Road, authentic Cockney singing every Friday night, room above open for private parties. On several occasions, we have awoken in the middle of the night – my good lady wife, Beryl, that is . . . '

'Cheese,' said Beryl, arranging a ringlet, and laying a hand on her cleavage.

' . . . awoken to the unmistakable roar of sawn-off shotguns, and realised some poor bleeder was copping his lot.'

The typewriters rattled behind me, and the flashbulbs popped; I sensed that, perhaps through fear of involvement, perhaps through community pride, the man was holding something back.

'Would you say,' I enquired tastefully, 'that there was a connection between these shootings and the high wages earned by today's youth, the violence on those TV programmes unrecommended by the responsible Sunday critics, the breakdown of understanding between police and public

24

due to such blots on our copybook as the Sheffield beatings, the decline of pop groups, and the filthy local housing which is the legacy of the Tory government?'

'Yes,' said the landlord. 'You may quote me on that.'

We gathered up our gear, satisfied, and moved on. Ned Tryste, teenage pioneer of hand-held typewriter techniques, nudged me significantly. 'The man's a natural!' he whispered.

Outside, down an alley, I found Ferdy, my assistant, arranging two negroes in front of a wall bearing the legend 'Spades Clear Out!' I set my aperture tensely. This was the real stuff.

'Look at the swastikas, for Chrissake!' shouted Ferdy, scattering some broken bottles round their feet, 'and stop that bloody irresponsible grinning.'

I finished the roll, just as a young copper came round the corner. The team fell on him.

'I imagine the police are baffled?' I said.

'We expect to make an arrest soon,' said the constable. 'But this is a perfectly ordinary crime, gentlemen. The work of teenaged hotheads and . . .'

'Ordinary?' I cried, and we all cackled fitfully, while I took a close-up of the copper's bulging truncheon pocket silhouetted against the peeling signboard of a local school. 'Do you realise that today's teenagers were raised in the atmosphere of failure attendant upon the collapse of the ground-nut scheme? Do you not understand that many of them were reaching puberty during the Suez crisis? That Tory affluence has now provided them with the wherewithal to buy shooters?'

The copper shrugged, moved on, defeated by reason, and, at the moment, the lunchtime sirens began to wail. We moved like lizards, into a position behind a wall opposite a factory exit. The workers began to file out, their grainy London faces rich telephoto fodder; here they were, the living background, the setting made flesh in which the young hooligans had grown up, with nothing to look up to but their elders' penury. It was a moving sight, and our eyes were misty behind our rangefinders; it was all we could do to capture a few quick single-shots before the men got into their cars and drove off.

And then, as if by a miracle, they appeared. A group of kids – they couldn't have been more than twelve years old –

came into sight. They were shouting in an abandoned, care-less, and – yes – a rebellious manner. And they were carry-ing catapults. I nudged Ferdy.

'My God!' I whispered. 'They're . . .'

'I know, I know,' he said, under his breath. 'It's Sub-teenagers!'

I stepped up to them.

'Where are you off to, then, lads?' I said brightly.

They eyed me with backstreet cunning.

'Gonna go offan kill rats inna cellars!' said one.

I nudged Ferdy again.

'Hear that? "Kill rats"! By, they're fly, these people. Pray God that Cockney wit never dies.'

'The very woof of our culture would be irreparably torn,' said Ferdy, typing furiously.

I turned back to the boys. I can be sly, too.

'Bet that catapult could kill someone, eh?' I said.

One of them sniffed.

'Gotter ittim inis eye,' he said. 'You're offa the papers, 'ncha? My bruvver's gotta pitcher you took of 'im kicking a bloke in Margit stuck up onnis wall. 'E's bin kicking blokes all over the Souf Coast ever since so's you could do 'im in colour, only your never come back, didja?'

'You read the papers, then?' I said.

'Only stickup the pitchers,' said the boy. 'I like them pitchers of blokes punching uvver blokes' 'eads in. I mean, it's real, 'n'it?' A canny glaze slid across his eyes. 'You wanna picher of me kickin' Jimmy Potter innis fork?'

It was too good to be true. We shot them in their crum-bling school playground, against an old, torn Conservative campaign poster, outside a cinema showing *Lord Of The Flies*, and we even managed to find a house scheduled for demolition, where we could pose them on the steps, looking unwanted.

When they'd gone, we were silent for a bit. Then Ferdy turned to me. 'There's nothing *quite* like the thrill of a real scoop, is there, old man?'

'Nothing,' I said quietly. 'The ones that really get you deep down inside.' I shouldered my Ikoblitz, and set my jaw. 'It only happens in Fleet Street,' I said.

The Decline and Fall
of Madame Butterfly

The Japanese today offer their ladies services which must be unique in all the world. The demand for these services arose from the war, the occupation, and the introduction of western standards of female attractiveness. In Tokyo . . . a quick and usually painless operation will remove the young lady's Mongolian fold; more sophisticated surgery can make her eyes less oriental looking . . . more delicate plastic surgery can reshape a nose entirely, raising it generally and narrowing the nostrils to a Caucasian pattern. Large breasts have become an asset. . . .

New Statesman

With an easy nonchalance born of four parts gin, one part vermouth, I tied a makeshift clove-hitch in my safety-belt. As the jet banked smoothly into saffron cloud, I nudged the man beside me.

'Smell that?' I said. 'Orange blossom, that is. Jasmine. Joss sticks.'

He turned to me, slowly. He'd been asleep ever since boarding at Calcutta. I couldn't help a stifled snigger as I took in the rude lineaments of British unsophistication, the check plastikap, the mildewed Norfolk jacket, the knobbly stick, the threadbare plus-fours, and the red neck, lined with Sussex experience, poking out from the Aertex shirt. He smiled, obviously shy.

'By heavens!' I cried, craning across him towards the window, 'you can hear the paddles chunking, mate! Can you imagine what's going on down there? The temple bells clanging away like nobody's business, the seething oriental backstreets, the coolies scoffing the old egg foo yong, the voluptuous geishas limbering up in the communal bathhouses . . .'

He shrugged, tapping his crusty briar against a mudstained gaiter, affecting a pitiful carelessness in his attempt to impress me. Not that one could blame him; my travelstained Aer Lingus bag, veteran of two flights across the storm-tossed Irish Sea, my Austin Reed lightweight tropical suit, the 'London-Tokyo' label hanging proudly around my neck, all proclaimed the seasoned credentials of the Jet Set, of which my honest rustic companion could, alas, only dream. What capricious whim of fate could have yoked us together, he a solid English yeoman, I the impeccable owner of a new Giant Filthmaster washing-machine and a six-day free trip to the Korean Riviera?

We slid out from the dissolving cloud.

'There it is!' I cried, 'Tokyo!'

My companion examined a battered gold Hunter.

'The dlagonfly will be alighting on the gleen loof,' he murmured. 'The golden apples of the sun are lipe. The klingfisher awaits the lising gnat.'

'I beg your pardon?' I said.

'Welcome to Tokyo,' he said, handing me his card. It read:

NIGEL CHOY
The Laburnums,
Acacia Road,
Tokyo 4.

He touched his forelock, and vanished into the customs shed, a large tin building with a cardboard façade cut in the shape of Westminster Abbey. A nice touch, I thought, for tourists. I glanced up from my luggage to find myself looking down at Cary Grant.

'Mr. Grant!' I cried. 'May I say how much my wife and I admire . . . I say, have you always been five feet tall?'

'Please lead the card,' said Cary Grant. For the first time I noticed his blue uniform and braided cap. 'No tlansistor ladios, no camelas, no dangerous dlugs?'

'By the right!' I shouted. 'Sessue Hayakawa to the life! I never knew you did impressions. You ought to be in pictures.'

28

We both laughed uproariously. That's what I like about showbiz people. All heart. He put a chalkmark on my case, confiscated my watch, and, still laughing, threw me out. I stood on the lush paper lawns in front of the airport, feeling myself really in Japan for the first time. I had twenty-four hours to kill before making my Korean connection. The East lay at my feet.

'Excuse?' said a mellifluous voice at my knee.

'Good Lord! What brings you to this neck of the woods?'

'You want good hotel, mister?' said Arthur Askey. 'Good bed, plenty home cooking, loast beef, bakewell tart, leasonable lates?'

We leapt aboard a 653 trolleybus, mingling, strangely unnoticed, with the oriental hordes. At the back of the bus sat crowds of locals, slant-eyed, pig-tailed, kimonoe-ed, kept in their places by a tiny relative of George Sanders who quietened any rebelliousness with a crack of his miniature bullwhip. At the front of the bus sat a strange agglomeration of weeny Westerners, three Albert Finneys, four Audrey Hepburns, and a sad-looking woman with Quintin Hogg's face and great pendulous breasts. I whispered in Arthur Askey's ear. 'What goes on here?'

'The shadow of democlacy falls on the navel of Buddha,' he replied, with that Liverpudlian frankness which has endeared him to millions. 'Tennyson he say: Better fifty years of Europe than a cycle of Cathay. Olientals must learn: West is Best. Beauty is in the eye of shareholder.'

The bus stopped opposite a plinth on which the recently imported Venus de Milo stood, surrounded by a crowd of keening women, many of whom were stripped to the waist, revealing, among other things, their horribly mutilated arms. I followed Askey to a large peeling mock-Tudor hotel; several beefeaters were ambling about the courtyard, playing a selection from *Desert Song* on their bagpipes. I went inside, and Konrad Adenauer, clad in Yale sweatshirt and Black Watch kilt rushed towards me.

'Welcome to Legent Palace Hotel!' he shouted. 'Hoping stay will be happy one, no coming in after ten o'clock, please not to take towels on beach and oblige, what time morning cuppa?'

I signed in, while the Duke of Gloucester took the bags to my room. It was a large vault, painted dark-brown, containing a brass bed, a basketwork armchair, a 19th century escritoire, a cracked water jug, two china shepherdesses, a reproduction of 'The Gleaners', a Gideon Bible, and two barbola chamber pots. The window looked out over rows of semi-detached paper houses stretching away towards the Albert Memorial. A vague malaise settled on me. I went down to the bar, bent on a quick *sake* before tackling my *moo goo gai pan*; the barman smiled deprecatingly and pointed out that this was a Watney's house. I tried to placate him by praising his performance in 'On the Waterfront', but he drew his inscrutability about him, and slid noiselessly away. When the Luton Girls' Choir started telling the story about the Chinaman and the farmer's daughter, I went into dinner, where the head waiter, in the nicest way possible, turned down my demand for chop sticks, mainly because he was afraid of lowering the tone of the place, but also because they aren't much use when it comes to fish fingers and charcoal-broiled tripe.

The meal over, I wandered into downtown Tokyo, clad in luminous shantung tuxedo, dark glasses, and two-tone Neapolitan hushpuppies, waiting for the local exotica to cast aside their *cheong-sams* and incinerate themselves in my gemlike flame. After three hours, I found myself hunched over a glutinous cappucino, chewing the fat with Gracie Fields, accumulated at the nearby Locarno after a singularly depressing Paul Jones in which I was constantly partnered by Alma Cogan in a variety of summer frocks. All desire gone, I turned to Gracie, and, my vestigial lust turned now to idle curiosity, I said:

'Tell me, Gracie, you're a nice Japanese kid, I can talk to you – this is only from academic interest, but there's a question I'd like to ask . . . '

She smiled, scrutably, as one long used to such inquiries, and shook her head. Silver threads glittered among the gold.

'So solly,' she said, 'no truth in story. Solly to disappoint.'

'That's all right,' I said. 'I just thought I'd ask.'

Memoirs from the
House of the Dead

Lately, the presses have groaned beneath the newsprint devoted to sob-stories of British tourists who've fallen foul of a hostile Continong. But much is left to explain.

Tuesday, 10th.

They came for K. this morning. A little before dawn, I think; hard to tell, because no window, but I heard firing-squad coming off night-shift, marching down corridor. K. and I had been taking turns at spitting on last night's crust and were getting it in near-edible state when they threw back bolts, unchained K. from ceiling, and dragged him out by his lower lip. He was damned good about it. When you get to Dover, he said, have a small bitter for me. Tell Milly to prune the roses. He smiled. I heard them all in the court-yard; my Flemish is pretty ropey, but words for parking-offence came over clearly enough in indictment; familiar by now. Heard K. refuse blindfold, too.

Prisoner next door has begun knocking on drain. Hysterical; can't manage to decipher anything.

Wednesday, 11th.

Apparently British Ambassador has been sending stiff notes. Am now allowed to hang right way up on wall. Digestion better. Still concerned over rats who have now come up with plan for pyramid which brings them within six inches of left foot. Guards arrived after lunchtime bean and beat me with rhino whips. Continued to protest ignorance of law prohibiting open shirt to Englishmen visiting public monu-

31

ments in Brussels, but to no avail; not permitted interpreter, and guards not allowed to understand French, since live wrong side of demarcation line.

Prisoner next door continues to knock on drain, but has controlled himself. Morse not my strong suit, but appears he challenged head waiter over bill. Last year. Headstrong fool.

Thursday, 12th.

Visited by priest this morning, who took away my teeth. Now have no defence against encroaching rats. Beginning to feel guilty of something; inevitable. Wish there was something in my life I did wrong and got away with. Can't think of anything.

Wonder if Miranda made it to the Swiss border? Probably didn't even get through Germany; believe radiator hit in two places. Pity not driving Volkswagen; if ever get out of this, shall draft strong letter suggesting abolition of GB plate.

Stroke of luck this afternoon. Cell block commandant turns out to be Dutchman I saved at Arnhem; recognised me by withered left arm (shrapnel). Long pleasant chat about old times. In consequence (I feel), beatings reduced to one a day.

Prisoner next door broke drain, and was garrotted.

Friday, 13th.

Exercise day. Allowed to run gauntlet of gendarmes. In between rounds, opportunity to exchange notes with F. He was member of Consulate staff thrown in Zeebrugge ship canal by enraged citizens for scratching in street. Pulled out four miles downstream by police, summarily thrashed, and formally accused of polluting inland waterway. When jailed, complained of being beaten with own wooden leg; thereupon confined to sewers. Splendid chap, bears no grudges. Mystified by decay of British image, though. New draft of prisoners arrived in compound. During half-hour break while gendarmes rested, new man, Scot, natural leader, three-year stretch for failing to tip, attempted to organise escape committee. Formulated plan for escaping in stolen gendarme's uniform. Several prisoners fainted at suggestion. Disgusting lack of proper spirit. Nevertheless, two men who had already effected three successful escapes from English holiday camps expressed enthusiasm. Cannot participate myself, since diet seems to be affecting eyes.

Guards brought Red Cross food parcel this evening, but had decency not to eat it in front of me.

Saturday, 14th.

Woken during night by persistent animal roars in court-yard. Learned at morning beating that escape aborted. Wonder where they got hold of lions? Got to hand it to these people – may not go along with their methods, but they're damned efficient. Hope England aware of their territorial ambitions.

Dragged up to Room 101 this afternoon. Am getting used to electrodes now; doctors all very kind.

Feelings of guilt increased strongly this evening. Ignorance of law no excuse. Found self saying this over and over. After all, wouldn't go to Glyndebourne in pyjamas; criminal negligence not to wear tie in front of flower of Flemish womanhood.

Sunday, 15th.

Amazing progress. Unshackled from wall, and allowed to crouch on table. Commandant not a bad egg at all. Job not made any easier by fools trying to escape all the time.

Beatings to be cut to one every two days. Some prisoners apparently complaining of preferential treatment; shall see to it they get what they deserve. Bloody foreigners. Give 'em the rhino whip.

Monday, 16th.

Fed.

Tuesday, 17th.

Staggered to learn am going to be repatriated. Being kept only till doctors feel completely satisfied with my fitness. Nothing to do with efforts of Ambassador, who is tool of reactionary insular government, but due entirely to Flemish hosts. Shall be sorry to leave them. Time here not altogether wasted, however. Have learned much; astonishing how travel broadens mind.

Am sickened at prospect of returning to Sheffield. But man goes where duty directs. Much to do, little time. Shall start small and work up. Introduction of rhino whips would be a good beginning.

3

Suffer Little Children

Somewhere, far off, the weekend died on a midnight chime. My wife gathered up the shredded remains of the Sunday papers.

'You haven't touched your colour supplement,' she said.

'I didn't fancy it.'

'Sheer waste. After all the trouble they've gone to. You should be ashamed – am I expected to throw it away now, when four-fifths of the world's population can't get enough to read?' She ripped out a dazzling page. 'Look – just have a bit of Mountbatten. Or one of these delicious adverts. Just a paragraph or two?'

'I couldn't manage a thing,' I said.

She glared icily at me, and moved away. There was a tiny hissing sound as she dropped an aspirin into a vase of chrysanthemums. It sank gently to the bottom, bumped the agglomeration of old green pennies, ball-bearings, shrapnel and other rejuvenating junk, and began to dissolve, slowly.

'You've been at the Epilogue again,' she said. 'I can tell. You have that expression of intolerable guilt on your face. The one with the spaniel eyes and the flabby lip. I suppose they were talking about the decay of faith in a Thermonuclear Age?'

I didn't answer. The flowers shed a few shrivelled petals, pessimistically.

'They don't make chrysanthemums like they used to,' said my wife.

'What do you suppose becomes of all the children?' I said.

'When?'

'After the admen have finished with them. After they've served their purpose.'

She glided to the door. 'I'm going to run a bath,' she said. 'I hope you get it all worked out.'

Easily said. She has a poor grasp of despair, that girl. And all those tinies going to the wall. I closed my eyes tight, until all I could see was that peculiar Persian carpet pattern that seems to be tattooed on the inside of my eyelids. But it wasn't around for long – it faded, and They began to appear, materialising out of the gloom, little faces upturned in supplication for a bowl of porridge, little mouths stuffed with frozen fish fingers, little hands clutching chocolate peanuts that refused to melt in them, little feet stomping Mummy's brain until it cried out for the relief dispensed only by the tablet which nothing acts faster than. There were children patting dogs enriched with marrowbone jelly, and children having hysterics over the *TV Times*, and children gorging themselves on glucose drinks and leaping from deathbeds, and children standing pitifully at garden gates praying that God wouldn't let Mummy forget the fruit gums. Thousands of little faces. The faces of the innocent damned. The faces that launch a thousand consumer goods. The kids from the ads.

I opened my eyes to escape. Who are they? Where do they come from? And, more to the point, where do they go?

Once upon a time, and a very recent time it was, there was a small, sickly-sweet coterie of creatures called Child Actors. They were born of a virgin union between Freddie Bartholomew and Shirley Temple, and wet-nursed by cinemoguls who knew a good thing when they saw it. These tinies inhabited a specific dramatic compound, bordered on one side by the territory of Wee Georgie Wood and Jimmy Clitheroe, and on the other by Rin Tin Tin and Francis the Talking Mule. Like them, they were a type of freak, whose dramatic roles were either irrelevant, or at best created for them simply because they *were* children. As Sam Johnson remarked of such performing beasts, audiences marvelled not at how well they acted, but rather at the sheer fact of their doing it at all. And the stuff they belted out, the *Little Lord Fauntleroys* and *Little Colonels*, were unashamed make-believe and preposterous charade. Also, the kids seemed fully aware that the whole business was a bit of a giggle, and, but for the occasional inflated ego, they all seem to have come through reasonably unscathed. Since all children are dab hands at play-acting, it couldn't have been too difficult to maintain the separation between real and celluloid life, and at the end of the day they no doubt hung up their cowboy suits, in just the same way as their amateur contemporaries, and, pausing for a forkful of spinach and a paternal lecture on spitting, toddled off to bed to dream of becoming a fireman.

But how could one possibly hope for a similar normality being the lot of the diminutive thespians who for the past few years of commercial telly have been putting their hearts and souls into flogging raspberry jelly to the gluttons in front of the little blue screens? How can they manage to distinguish between art (for want of a better word) and reality? What, to the weeny, unformed mind, is the difference between tellymummy and real Mummy, what is the difference between having to learn that Jesus is meek and mild, but then so is Fabulous Sludgo Toilet Soap? There's no problem for a hardened adult actor who grins bravely through a whiteness test, then nips round smartly to the four-ale bar where he sends the whole thing up rotten. He knows, after all, that the whole shebang is a con-game, above all that he is *acting* it, and that it has nothing to do with life away from the cameras.

One can hardly imagine that the kids make similar adjustments. I have yet to stroll into an ITV cafeteria to find a bunch of cynical five-year-olds propping up the counter and weeping into their orangeades about how they could right this minute be playing the lead in *Peter Pan*, if only they'd had the breaks, or laughing fit to bust over the fact that they'd just told a Yogi Bear captive audience that it would grow up big and strong like Daddy if only it stuck to a diet of Cracklepops. No. Half the kids one sees in the commercials are no more than six or seven, and it's inevitable that they should believe implicitly not only in the stuff they're purveying, but also in the ethic that gives it life. I have seen a year-old mite, sloshing blancmange deliriously over himself and his tellyparents, and repeating the name of the product again and again. God knows what its real parents do when the agency pram delivers the infant back to them, and they try to persuade it that food is not meant to be flung on the ceiling, or try to teach it to say something other than 'Globbo Custard' during its formative years. And *you* try persuading a swaddled infant that you're its real mummy and daddy, and the nice people who let it sling grub about are only actors.

It's difficult to imagine that real parents would allow their offspring to go off on a big alienation kick, out into a wide and predatory adworld to be adapted and shaped by commercial hands, and turned into a human parrot to preach the gospel according to Kittyfood. The more I think about it, the more likely it seems that these children are actually bred for the purpose. Somewhere on the other side of England, perhaps, in a great windowless warehouse swathed in the mist of the fens, and painted a drab khaki, handpicked admen are breeding and multiplying, scattering their maker's image through the land; the tinies are snatched away at birth and used to propagandise rubber teats and plastic baths, taught to smile and gurgle until they grow teeth, and are weaned on to strained food ads. As soon as they can walk, they toddle towards the cameras, holding out sweets and jams to beckoning ad-uncles, nine hours a day, five days a week, and are locked in insulated cells at sunset. Gradually, in special underground schools, they will be taught to mouth ecstasies over steaming soup-bowls, to reproach nine-till-five mummies for not using ZXK $4\frac{1}{2}$ in their toothpaste, to fly into the arms of homecoming daddies who bear dummy cartons of chocolates, and to sing stirring patriotic jingles about cellular vests. As age comes on, as it must, they will be trained to subsist on charcoal-filtered fags and gin, they will be introduced to girls on fresh spring days, and wrenched apart from them at nightfall, they will be sent out in lifeboats, dropped by parachute, sent up sheer rock-faces in pursuit of a view and a bar of chocolate, plunged under water with ball-point pens, and buried alive with shockproof watches. And eventually they will dodder like worn-out machines into an inevitable senility, to claim that ninety years of Swillo Fruit Salts made them what they are today.

And, naturally, we'll all believe them.

Agentes Provocateuses

A former Jugoslav showgirl who was granted political asylum in the U.S. after leaving Cuba in 1960 was reported today to have been a leading madam of a call-girl ring which specialised in operations at the United Nations building. A Hungarian blonde who is a familiar figure at the U.N. headquarters, and a Peruvian prostitute living in Manhattan are also being sought for questioning. Agents of the F.B.I. who are investigating the activities of so-called 'corridor girls' at the United Nations, regard them as very important witnesses.

The Daily Telegraph

(*A large office at the top of U.N. building. Apple-green suedette wallpaper, tangerine deep-pile carpet, a night-blue ceiling showing the astronauts in their courses. On the far wall, a map of uptown Manhattan dotted with coloured flags and tiny red plastic hearts. At a low desk sit an M.I.5 man and an F.B.I. man; behind them stands a multilateral guard, a Vietnamese half-caste in Black Watch kilt, West Point T-shirt, turban, jackboots, and a Sandhurst tie. He carries a halberd.*)

M.I.5 . . . so I said puce was too *bold* for the ceiling and he said the Regency Stripe made the office look a tiny bit Wembley and you had to have a dramatic contrast what with the muted scatter-rugs and I said I didn't think bold puce was me *at all* but then he said . . .

(*A knock at the door. The guard shouts an order in pidgin Esperanto and the door opens to admit a trolley pushed by a withered crone shielding her face with one arthritic hand.*)

F.B.I.: Coffee, thank God! Suk!

(*The guard steps forward, tastes the coffee, and steps back. The two men drink. The crone retires noiselessly.*)

F.B.I.: Poor bitch; What a story that makes for the files, Charlie – Ziegfeld Follies to the Diplomatic Corps. The only surviving member of the League of Nations soubrettes without portfolio. Strictly a pro; a real trouper. They sure broke the mould when they made her.

M.I.5: Eheu fugaces! And as it comes to this? (*Waves a sheaf of papers and publicity photographs, and throws them down disgustedly*). A flock of vibro-masseuses, unemployed models, screenless starlets – dear God, the whole of counter-espionage sticks in the craw! Ou sont les . . .

F.B.I. (*Savagely*): Lousy bunch of goddam amateurs! Lord knows, Charlie, without your impression of Mae West, and the Under-secretary's 'Little Yellow God', the last Security Council Annual Outing would've been the flop of all time.

M.I.5: Worst of it is, I'm beginning to get *mean* over investigating them, Bernie. Used to be an absolute *hoot*. I can excuse anyone as long as they've got a bit of originality, a spot of *colour*, d'you see? Take Zazu Wurlitzer . . .

F.B.I.: The plaything of the International Bank?

M.I.5: The very same. Terribly naughty of her to have had the Nike-Zeus firing-circuit tatooed on her abdomen just before she defected, but it was done with – a *panache* that just isn't there any more.

F.B.I.: Right! And you had to forgive her; she only did it to spite De Georgio for promising Icelandic fishing-rights to his Yemeni housegirl in return for the mock-up of the Uzbekistan radar sites she'd found in the warming-pan of the Bulgarian third secretary.

M.I.5: Damn' clever, actually, that Bulgar. Turned out he'd been in the UNESCO lav writing a piece for *Krokodil* satirising himself and recommending his resignation ironically, when he looked up and noticed the Arabic graffiti; these were actually an anagram on the name of the Dutch girl who cleans the telephones in the I.L.O. waiting-room. She'd been picked up on the subway by our man in Tashkent, who was in fact a counter-counter-spy in the pay of the Reds. Temporarily, anyhow. That's how the Bulgar got hold of the plans.

F.B.I.: Harry H. God, quel esprit de corps!

M.I.5 (*looks at him askance*): Hallo! Didn't realise you spoke foreign lingoes, old man.

F.B.I. (*taps his nose cannily*): Officially, I don't.

(*They roar helplessly for several seconds. A buzzer interrupts them.*)

M.I.5: Oh, Lord, that must be the first examinee. Suk, let her in.

(*Enter a pneumatic teenage blonde in a sheath dress of printed cotton patterned with blueprints marked Secret, Top Secret, and Most Secret over the appropriate parts of her anatomy. She twinkles on needle heels to a low chair before the desk, and hikes up her skirt. The F.B.I. man leaps forward and plucks a roll of microfilm from her tricolour garter. He and the M.I.5 man inspect it closely, and burst into hysterical giggling.*)

F.B.I.: Delegate Orminski! Who'd have thought the old sonofabitch had it in him?

Girl: They send him monkey-glands under plain cover.

M.I.5 (*quickly*): Who do?

Girl: His fambly. They don't half worry about 'im. His mum don't like to see 'im go wivout nuffink.

F.B.I.: Looks like she can stop worrying. (*He divides the film and each man puts a half in his wallet. They exchange grins.*) Now, Miss Fludd, we'd like to ask you a coupla questions. First...

Girl: I don't 'ave to answer nuffink. I got diplomatic immunity. I know me rights. I've 'ad to speak to 'em about opening me letters, an' all; any more of that, and I'll 'ave the whole bleeding lot of you back looking after the carpark.

M.I.5 (*agitatedly*): Good grief, it's nothing like that ... (*Smiles ingratiatingly*) ... Beryl. We'd just like to check on a silly report we've had from some nosey old thing in the I.M.F. office about one or two teeny expenses he's traced to you. After all, the Fund *has* given away $6,265,000,000 over the past few years, and the clerks are getting a bit bolshie over office economies. I'm sure you understand. Now, what's all this about a £400,000 Neo-Babylonian folly on Richmond Hill?

Girl: I've 'ad to move Mum out of 'er penthouse. She 'as giddy turns. But she likes a view, see?

M.I.5: I do, indeed. But I *do feel* . . .

Girl: I come from a broken 'ome. (*Voice cracks.*) Till I was fourteen, I lived in constant fear of 'aving to work for a living . . . (*She breaks down and sobs. The F.B.I. man comforts her vigorously. He looks up.*)

F.B.I.: God, Charlie, it's a lousy world to bring a kid into!

M.I.5: Poor child. (*He puts a match to the dossier. Exit girl.*)

F.B.I.: Pity we didn't get around to asking her about that airmail copy of *Pravda* she left in the Acapulco-Hilton; the one with the Polaris fuelling system sketched on it in eyebrow pencil.

M.I.5 (*despondently*): What's the use? She'd only have denied it, and then where would we have been? Lots of fiddly paperwork and stuff, and with the GATT croquet tournament coming off next week, I'd never have found the time. By the way, old chap, are you turning out for us?

F.B.I.: Sorry, Charlie, can't make it. As of last night, I'm ineligible. (*He takes off his jacket to reveal an M.V.D. uniform. On the left breast he wears the Order of Lenin.*)

M.I.5: I *say*! Bottle-green! It does suit you, Bernie. (*Suddenly glum.*) But this really is a bit off, you know. We'll have to field that blonde idiot from Interpol. And I *hate* left-handers. Can't trust 'em an inch.

F.B.I.: Hate to do it to ya, Charlie. But a buy's gotta eat. (*Puts on overcoat, turns up collar.*) Well, I guess it's dojzvidanya.

M.I.5: Sadly, old man, sadly. (*He extends his hand.*) Good hunting. Don't take any wooden kopecks.

(*They laugh, and shake hands. Exit the F.B.I. man. M.I.5 turns to the guard.*)

M.I.5: Just for a handful of silver he left us, just for a riband to stick in his coat (*Suk smiles orientally. M.I.5 blows his nose.*) Ah well, so geht es. (*He picks up the telephone.*) Get me Captain Nyakov . . . Hallo, Fyodor? . . . Look, put a tail on Bernie Griswold . . . I don't think he's going to be with us long, tovarich . . . No, strictly a New Hampshire deviationist . . . Cheerio.

(*The buzzer rings again. Suk admits a svelte brunette swad-*)

dled in chinchilla. *She takes off her sunglasses, glowers at M.I.5.*)

M.I.5. (*thumps the desk*): Dammit, Gretchen, I've told you never to come here!

Girl: Donnerwetter! Some lousy business-manager you out to be turned! For twenty-five per cent and first choice of my cast-off dresses, better from you I expect. The I.T.U. counter-counter-counter-spies have between me and our Mother Superior in Ecuador a message intercepted. Endlich – our convent in the Bronx raided was, und eighteen novices awaiting shipment to Quito into custody taken were.

M.I.5: Lord Almighty! We've got ten minutes to make the submarine at Hoboken! (*He grasps her hand, and they disappear into the dumb-waiter. The rumble of the pulley echoes in the darkening room. Suk stands there alone, motionless, for a long time. Then, very, very cautiously, he begins to change sex.*)

Uneasy Lies the Bust

Since the majority of men have three-dimensional vision, but only two-dimensional appreciation of whatsoever things are noble and of good report, the assurance that beauty is only skin-deep is pretty cold comfort to a flatchested heart of gold. Yet I wonder how many of those maidens who grudgingly concede that beauty is at the very least subcutaneous have ever reflected upon the liability of a Bust?

Not one of your run-of-the-mill, girl-in-the-street busts, you understand. But such a Bust as dreams – male and female alike – are made of, the sort of item advertised by the London School of Fatty Degeneration, or whatever those joy-factories are called that promise immediate redistribution of Precious Inches and pledge themselves to the annihilation of warts. (Not that you should believe all you read in the Tube; most of the before-and-after picture of Mrs. A. of Stockport suggests that Our Highly Trained Staff consists mainly of touching-up artists. Either that or Mrs A. spent four months locked in the basement with a packet of Ryvita until her whole body shrank, leaving only the bust standing.) Once or twice in a generation, a Bust like this is born, *sui generis*; but its life, along with those of queens and pools winners, is not the beer-and-skittles deal of popular legend. Complex factors are involved, not the least of which is the problem of living up to the growth on your chest; usually, the growth itself takes command, like a Ionesco sideboard, until you're merely the vehicle for lugging it from place to place. How often does one hear starlets complain that they might have been something more than cannon-fodder for

Sid James, if only someone had taken their Bust seriously? It's an uphill road from *Carry On Nurse* to *Hedda Gabler*; you have to fight for every inch.

A ripe field for the perceptive sociologist, this; but one aspect is of particular interest. Insurance. You, battle-hardened by *Today in Parliament*, may have been quick to excoriate the star who insures her Bust as a publicity-seeking hypocrite exploiting the Norwich Union for her own ends. Ours is a faithless, cynical age; too many people are ready to condemn a Bust out of hand. They do not see that a Bust is an ideogram of human frailty; its rise and fall might be written up as The Parable Of A Thousand Natural Shocks, a lesson in mortality and a warning against *hubris*. In the morning it is green, and groweth up, but in the evening it is cut down, dried up, and withered. On a Bust, doom hangs heavy. Accident, structural deterioration, a change of fashion, will see its owner on the skids for good. Which is why insurance against both sudden and gradual disaster is essential; but what a sordid business it must be for the Bust and its curator.

Take the sudden-accident angle first: assessing the relative values of parts of the body is never a pleasant task; there's nothing grislier than those two-bob policies obtainable from airport slot-machines:

In the event of injury sustained in transit the Company will compensate the injured as set out below

LOSS OF ONE LEG	£250
LOSS OF TWO LEGS	£450
LOSS OF ONE EAR	£100

and so on. Just as your flight-number's called, a revolting vision materialises of yourself as claimant, standing in a line of mutilated groaners, a man with his thumb in a jam-jar, a dog on crutches, an old woman with no ears. Behind the grille, hundreds of clerks sit sorting out photographs of amputated feet and putting fivers into envelopes. 'Good morning, sir. The stewardess poked your eye out, sir? The left one. I see. You don't happen to have the eye with you, sir? Splendid! I trust a cheque will do, the Templehof disaster's left us a bit short . . .' How much more wretched to have to claim on a damaged Bust; since the figure involved is usually around $1,000,000, you can be certain the insurance boys aren't going to cough up without an intensive examination of the circumstances. One wonders whether a Bust-policy is as depressing to fill in as a house-insurance; is the owner suddenly made aware of all the terrible things that can happen? Does she imagine the Bust involved in storm, flood, tempest, civil commotion or labour disturbance? Will it one day be the victim of an act perpetrated by malicious persons acting on behalf of or in connection with any political organisation? Will she see it damaged by aircraft and other aerial device or articles dropped therefrom, or put out of temporary/permanent use by impact with any road vehicle, horses, or cattle? What are the odds on its complete or partial destruction by a leakage of oil from any fixed oil-fired central heating system? Perhaps she gets on her knees every night, like the rest of us, to pray that it will never be caught up in civil commotion in Ireland, or imbroiled in War, Revolution, or Hostilities (whether War be declared or not), or contaminated following combustion of nuclear fuel, or – God forbid – that it will never be on the wrong end of an Act of God.

Maybe she doesn't. Accidents, after all, are things that happen to other Busts. What preys most on her mind is the process of Time; Bette Davis walks through her nightmares, cackling snatches from the *Dies Irae* in the livid glow of burning contracts. That million dollars is just a front, just one clause of a long-term policy the main function of which is to mature on the day the Bust does. At the end of ten years, barring accidents, she will tuck fifty grand into her superannuated cleavage, and get away from it all. But that brings other problems to mind.

Who gives her the idea of insurance? Maybe it's her agent, but all agents plagiarise their gimmicks from other sources. It's hard not to believe that the inspiration doesn't originally come from those notoriously enterprising salesmen, the Insurance Men themselves, the characters who trade on weakness and fear. Not a week goes by without some insidious voice chuntering away at me on the phone in what I can only describe as a tone of lugubrious optimism. Do I realise, he says, what a precarious business writing is? Do I also realise that none of us is getting any younger? There was even one swine from what must have considered itself to be an agency for the Smart Set who gleefully pointed out that since the age of 21, I'd been losing 500,000 brain cells per annum, and there weren't any more where those came from. I'm certain that these boys scour studio hand-outs and tabloids in the perpetual commission-hunt; once a victim is picked, they hound her to death. 'Do I have the great pleasure of speaking to Miss Deirdre Moue? Hi there! You don't know me, but I'm a great admirer of your, I mean of yours, I mean of you. I was looking through the *Daily Sketch*, see, and I couldn't help being struck by, I mean impressed with, I mean you have this *presence*, see? And what I'd like to say is, have you ever considered the precariousness . . . ' A couple of snide cracks about the ravages of time and what lies in store for golden lads and lassies, and the poor kid is hooked, thereafter to be bombarded in the post by strip-cartoon homilies describing This Vale Of Tears. You know the sort of thing – ill-drawn sequences of pictures showing moments in the life of an age-Bust. '*AT* 25 *I* (*we?*) *don't need insurance* – *AT* 35: *I* (*we*) *only wish I* (*we*) *carried insurance* – *AT* 45: *Without insurance I* (*we*) *don't know what is to become of me* (*us*).'

Being at best a non-practising atheist, I haven't unrolled the prayer-mat in a long time; but you can be sure that the next time I get around to it, I'll offer up a thank or two for the bust I haven't got. Somehow, the knowledge that I'll never be able to cash in on my own deterioration doesn't bother me too much.

You're Never Alone
with a Wine-Gum

It's one of the ironies of, among other things, life, that so little is known about the Central Office of Information. Most of us are *au fait* with the machinery and personalities of, say, the Ministry of Transport, or the Herring Industry Board, but next time you come up with a decent excuse to stop the average man in the street, ask him when he last thought about the C.O.I., and you may find yourself unpleasantly shocked.

It may be the name, of course. It has an alien metallic sound, an Orwellian flavour that makes the sensitive mind reject any temptation to dwell on it. Until very recently, I visualised the C.O.I. as a vast, windowless, pentagonal fortress, its grey concrete walls garnished with broken beer-bottles, its one iron door trellised with electrified barbed-wire; anyone unwise enough to pass by at midnight would hear the flagstones within echoing to the sounds of hobnails and alsatians. While inside, tiled labyrinths reeking of Lysol led to small, square rooms where men in dark glasses and rubber shoes watched computers digesting poetry, rewriting Hansard, censoring letters, tapping phone calls, listing subversives, and feeding information to sterilised secretaries in flat heels who copied everything down on green, silent, electric typewriters. In the lead-lined basement, Central Officers of Information were taught karate, Xosa, and how to make compasses out of betelnuts, before being paddled out to the Estuary in rubber dinghies and put aboard midget submarines. A week later, they would be squatting on their pinstriped haunches in the middle of the Kalahari, drawing maps in the sand with their umbrellas and explaining to tribesmen how to get to Wembley Park from Tottenham Court Road, and what to see at Hatfield House.

The sad thing about misconceptions like these is that their immaculacy can be shattered by the touch of the tiniest truth. This morning's papers carry news that the C.O.I. is to conduct an enquiry into the reasons why people continue to smoke 'despite repeated warnings of possible damage to their health'. Suddenly, one sees the C.O.I. full of sweet old men like Uncle Holly, shaking their snow-white heads wistfully at the follies of humankind, unable to face man's rejection of reason, all fouled up inside by the recognition that corrupted innocence is beyond redemption.

'We told them,' they murmur softly, 'but they hearkened not.'

The Senior Controller, a man who in his youth had been tipped for the Bishopric of Bath and Wells, but had forsaken all to become a C.O.I. mendicant friar (Grade II) wandering life's thorny byways, bringing Information to ignorant sinners, buries his kindly face in his hands, sighing, 'O wearisome condition of humanity!'

There's something genuinely pitiable in the assumption that people can be educated away from danger, or that evils can be cured solely by information. Is the C.O.I. shocked, one wonders, that there are still motorists on the roads, despite the rising accident-rates and M.O.T. propaganda? Are there C.O.I. missionaries on Saigon street-corners, handing out bi-lingual pamphlets explaining the correlation between bulletholes and infant mortality? Do C.O.I. family-planning experts pad through the teeming Bombay suburbs by night, beating on doors and shouting, 'Stop it, do you hear? STOP IT!' When last week the Australian delayed-drop parachutist plummeted to his death, was he followed down for ten thousand feet by a C.O.I. man shouting advice on how to give up the habit?

It's about time that the C.O.I. got it into its collective head that any propaganda campaign aimed at influencing the public's mind and behaviour must appeal not to reason, but to image. The admen learned years ago that a slogan like 'BUY SOAP – IT GETS YOU CLEAN!' never sold anything to anybody whereas a couple of lantern slides showing Cleopatra nipping out of a bubble bath and into history filled the streets with rioting housewives all screaming for a bar of Lifebuoy and a crack at the title. If the C.O.I. is genuinely concerned for public welfare, then they might as well know that any time or money spent on reporting the facts of lung cancer or button-holing nicotine slaves is abortive frittering.

The only way to have any effect on the adfed masses is to present an image of the smoker so loathsome and ridiculous that addicts would be ashamed to identify with it.

Not that it wouldn't be an uphill fight. The tobacco barons are old hands at the depth-psychology game and have left no cliché unturned in their establishment of the smoker-image as a man respected by men and adored by women. A man of the people, among whom his fliptop box and unwavering matchflame have become symbols of leadership and generosity, yet a man of deeper stuff withal, who may be found wandering the Embankment in trenchcoat and honest trilby, apparently alone but actually sunk in that romantic solitude known only to those who have shared the silent communion of man and weed. He is equally at home in the cockpit of a racing-car, fishing a trout stream in honest British waders, strolling along a beach with tuxedo and blonde blowing elegantly in the wind, or bolting scaffolding together in one of the great symbolic upward thrusts that discreetly characterise our Way of Life. From his lips, expect the unexpected; he may give off a subtle menthol flavour, reminiscent of Kanchenjunga, or the rich tang of smouldering peat. His eyes are always full of the lush satisfaction of empire builders and professional dancing partners.

The novitiate smoker is as hooked to this ego-ideal as he is to the cigarettes themselves, especially since the heroes of pop fiction tend to emerge from the same mould. My earliest experiments in the field involved a burnt-cork moustache, a pronounced swagger, and a penchant for sticking the dog-end in a corner of my mouth and drawling 'Frankly, Scarlett, I just don't give a damn,' through clenched teeth. I didn't break the habit until 1961, come to that. They'll have to sit up late at the C.O.I. to come up with a hero-substitute, but it could be done. What's needed is a saturation campaign of posters, films, strip cartoons, and so on, depicting the smoker as idiot, a neurotic incompetent who is always dropping ash down his partner's decolletage, stabbing people in the ear with a lighted cigarette, frustrating seducees by being struck down with a fit of hacking coughs at strategic moments, getting sparks in his eye halfway through a shaggy dog story, dropping his fag on the car floor just as the lights go green, and burning holes in hotel sheets. Gradually, his place in the ads would be overshadowed by the appearance of Captain Bullseye, a sweetsucking paragon who, in a series of interlinked soap-operas would course through high society in a liquorice haze, win the Grand Challenge Cup, climb Everest, breed a three-ton talking Aberdeen Angus, marry into the Royal Family, and stay in the Top Ten until next October, when he would be elected Liberal member for Marylebone.

Of course, a campaign like that would put a considerable strain on the kind old gentlemen in the C.O.I.; but at least it would keep them off the streets.

The Power and the Glory

Mr Denis Healey, the Minister of Defence, promised today that Britain would not lose her world lead in the development of vertical take-off aircraft.

B.B.C. News

The other morning, I was standing by the gas-stove, ears tensed for the first, fine, careless cackle of the percolator, and watching the new day creep feebly up the sky with that curious, droopy greyness that characterises February in London. The days, at this bleak time, never quite make it, never quite manage to look like anything but a dispirited pause between one night and the next. Buses loomed out of the dankness, shouldering the veils of drizzle aside rather in the manner of Akim Tamiroff pushing his way through the hanging beads of some Casablancan clip-joint, and disappeared back into the snivelling gloom. Not, all things considered, a morning designed to render the waking heart delirious at the prospect of unknown delights to come. But one, nevertheless, sadly appropriate to the island over which it had chosen to break.

We live on the first floor, which puts us on an exact level with the upper decks of London buses. Since our flat fronts the road, this means that at any given breakfast brew-up, people pass slowly by, in groups of thirty, and watch me with emotionless eyes as I strive to keep the front of my pyjamas closed; while I, in turn, stare back at them with the cool superiority of a man who in happier days might have been out chopping his way through Sikhs and Boers with terse Victorian purpose. These moments are about the only chance I have to show that breeding still counts, now that the Empire turns out to be something on which the sun never rises.

As, on this particular morning, we stood there, all thirty-one of us, I noticed for the first time a strange, unsettling sadness in the sixty alien eyes. They seemed to be looking to me for hope, for some mute sign that life was more than a tale told by an idiot; but before I could come up with a glance of comfort, a smile of faith, the bus moved on, and, wobbling slightly, they vanished into the gloom. I was deeply moved. The look was a look I had seen before, over the past few months, on faces passing in the street, in eyes across a public bar, in the brave, unflinching gaze of friends and cops and grocers, it was a look which said, with all the terrible expressiveness of silence, 'What is to become of us?'

I turned again to the percolator, which by this time seemed to be sobbing in sympathy with the general mood, and as I did so I caught the wheeze of the bedroom radio plucking weakly at the ether; my wife was awake, and avid for news. In these post-lapsarian days since the Tories shuffled brokenly into the sunset, England has been gripped by a feverish need for information unmatched since VE-Day. Each dawn, red eyes pop open all over the queendom, tiny, terrified stars in the overwhelming greyness, and wait for the eight a.m. news. In the preliminary silence, one seems to hear the creak of the economy, and the occasional subterranean groan of the trade-gap widening, like some glacier running between Land's End and John O'Groats and threatening to swallow us all; then comes the Greenwich Time Signal, followed by a B.B.C. voice intoning in old, noble accents the latest catalogue of horrors, the crash of stocks, the leaps of Bank Rate as it fights its way upstream, the rifts between and within political parties, the news that Britain has been bounced out of one more of the rooms in the fickle seraglio that is Europe today, stories of industrial dispute and international embarrassment, of crop failure and metal fatigue – the list seems endless. And, after it all, at ten minutes past eight, we drag ourselves pitifully from our beds with all-too-evident third rate power, and crawl away to work with the aforementioned look in our one hundred million eyes.

All right. I realise that many citizens of the United States, the Soviet Union, of France and Italy and Australia and Japan and all the rest of that gang of unprincipled upstarts currently touting their carpetbags around the market-places of the world and making the *Made in Britain* label an object of derision among men, I realise that these people, while sympathetic to our decline, tend to feel that we had a good run for everyone else's money, and that we're bitching unreasonably now that other flags want to get in on the act. Which is rather like tapping Billy Batson on the shoulder and saying 'Tough luck, Billy, but *Shazam* isn't the code word any more and we're not telling you what the new one is because we figure it's about time somebody else had a crack at the Captain Marvel title. Under the circumstances, our advice to you is to open a hardware store in Wichita Falls and leave Doctor Savannah to some of the younger fellahs.' Fair enough, unless you just happen to be Billy Batson, in which case you're stuck with a not inconsiderable problem of adjustment.

To return to specifics. I sloshed the coffee into a brace of Coronation Mugs, and, my upper lip a ridge of steel, padded into the bedroom to shore up my wife's wilting spirits with a few well-chosen words about the unconquerable will and study of revenge and similar snippets culled from our immortal heritage. She lay palely between the sheets, like one whose life has been frittered away on over-attention to camellias, listening to the newscaster reeling off reports of motions of censure on the Government, the wasting sickness of our gold reserves, the current protest march of aircraft workers, the latest lurch in the cost-of-living index, and other gobbets calculated to stick in the most optimistic craw. As the minutes flashed by, loaded to the gunwales with disaster, our commingled gloom deepened to a rich ebony, and I was on the point of hurling the radio through the window in the hope, perhaps, of felling a passing Volkswagen (a distinct statistical possibility), when the announcer paused suddenly, caught his breath, and said

'Mr. Denis Healey, the Minister of Defence, promised

today that Britain would not lose her world lead in the development of vertical take-off aircraft.'

There might have been more news after that, but we didn't hear it. My wife sat bolt upright in bed, the colour hurtling through her cheeks, her eyes uncannily bright, and clutched at my arm with that reserve of energy normally associated with drowning men in the presence of a sudden boathook.

'Can it be true?' she whispered.

I bit my lip.

'It has to be true,' I said.

'A world lead? Of our very own?'

'And we have it already!'

'Pray God we can hold on to it!' she muttered. We looked at one another with new hope. Horizons began to open before us, albeit vertically.

'I think – ' I said, very slowly, ' – I think it's all going to be all right, after all. I think we're going to come through.'

We drank our coffee in one draught, flung the cups over our shoulders, and offered a brief prayer for those in peril on the drawingboard. We had seen, at last, the thin end of the wedge, and it was a good wedge. Without a weapon of one's own, you see, without an original working weapon, it's impossible to hope for greatness. All very well to moan about defence expenditure and the lack of funds for schools, hospitals, pensions, roads, universities and all the rest of that pointless paraphernalia. All very well to brag about your Shakespeares and your Dantes and your Racines and your Ella Wheeler Wilcoxes. But when the chips are down, the chap from Smith and Wesson is the one we turn to. Weapons are the only true curators of our culture, and what in recent months has sapped the vitality of the Island Race has been the increasing doubt as to whether our independent deterrent was worth the sack it came in. While other nations proliferated their Polarises, or lobbed their I.C.B.M.'s willy-nilly between Novaya Zemlya and the Pole, we in Britain have gradually come to feel that the idea of having our own personal overkill was but an idle dream. We know that, called upon to swop punches with an Unnamed Foreign Power, we'd be hard put to to raise one mega-death among the lot of us. In all probability, the first day's hostilities would turn us into mere froth and flotsam; we should go down in history as no more than a patch of choppy water off the Irish coast. But not now. Now that we possessed a weapon in the development of which we led the world, to what glorious heights might we not rise?

'They ought to ring the churchbells,' said my wife, mopping her tears with a sheetcorner.

'By heavens!' I cried, smiting the mattress till the springs sang, 'The old lion lives to roar again! Let Russia tremble! Let China quail!'

My wife looked at the ceiling with passionate calm.

'And gentlemen in Osh Kosh, now a-bed
Shall think themselves accurs'd they were not here.
And hold their manhoods cheap . . .'

She lit a cigarette with a trembling flame. 'I say, my love, do you suppose it's too late to get the Empire back? Or, at least, some of the nicer bits?'

'Never!' I shouted. 'We are just entering the period familiarly known as the nick of time, and from here on in the going cannot be anything but good. Before the year is out, vertical take-off aircraft will be dropping like archangels all over the uncivilised world. Natives will run from the bush, crying "What is that great shining bird that drops from the skies like Ukkra, God of Sleet?" and we shall answer "It is a British vertical take-off aircraft, you heathen bastards, sent from the Great White Queen across the oceans, and you have ten seconds flat in which to start the grovelling routine."'

She clasped her hands ecstatically.

'Oh, think of it! There is trouble in the Straits . . . the natives are running riot through the rubber . . . mud has been thrown at the Flag . . .'

'. . . ten thousand miles away, a tall figure in mutton-chop whiskers hails a cab in Downing Street and clops rapidly . . .'

'Clops?'

'All right, roars. Roars rapidly through the night to Buckingham Palace . . . the Imperial Presence . . . the curt nods . . . the rasp of pen on parchment . . .'

'We have decided to send a vertical take-off aircraft!'

'Ah!'

'Ah!'

I strode to the window, hands clasped behind me, and looked into the coruscating future.

'What about this? De Gaulle criticises the movements of British hussars in the Sudan . . . our Ambassador hurries to Colombey-les-deux-Églises . . . the slap of glove on cheek . . . next morning, when the population of Marseilles awakes, there, bobbing on the tide, is a fleet of British vertical take-off aircraft . . .'

'Bobbing on the what?'

'I don't know why you have to quibble. Bobbing in the air, then. Shooting vertically up to five hundred feet, and shooting vertically down again, like great silver yo-yos, like . . . what's the matter?'

My wife was looking at me with every sign of fear.

'These vertical thingummies,' she said, quietly. 'What do they do except . . . except bob up and down?'

'What do you mean?'

'I mean, do they carry Ultimate Deterrents and stuff like that?'

'I suppose so.'

'But we haven't got any. Not anything Ultimate of our own.'

I said nothing. Something prickled against my tonsils.

'There isn't much percentage in just bobbing up and down, is there?' she said. 'Not unless you're in a position to improve on it. I mean, you're going to look pretty bloody ridiculous if in the middle of the yo-yo bit an Intercontinental What-not comes along horizon-tally and bowls you over like a row of skittles, aren't you?'

'They do fly on the level too, you know,' I said, with a scorn I was rapidly ceasing to feel.

'How fast?' she pressed.

'I don't know,' I said weakly. 'Quite fast, I suppose.'

'Fast *enough*?'

I looked down at the citizens romping about in the street below. There was a new bounce to their step, a new light in the communal eye. Here and there, a Union Jack fluttered. I turned away, pity and panic wrestling in my breast, to see her knuckles whitening on the edge of the blanket.

'It's all – it's all just another noble gesture, isn't it?' she whispered.

56

Slowly, I nodded. But the light, though waning fast, had not altogether passed from my eyes.

'All is not utterly lost, my love,' I said. 'One truth remains. When it comes to noble gestures, Britain still . . . '

'Leads the world?' she murmured.

'That's right,' I said.

The Word Game

The notion of an artist as a shaggy recluse living in an ivory tower is long out-of-date.
    From 'Investing in the Arts' (an Institute of Directors pub'n)

To: Arts Advisory Council
    Institute of Directors

                                        April 22nd, 1964

Gentlemen:

Allow me to congratulate you on your enterprise in uniting Art with Business, and in recognising that Art is too serious a game to be left to the artists. When you consider all those wasted centuries during which the priceless commodity of genius was left in the hands of long-haired, shiftless undesirables who couldn't give you change for a threepenny-bit, your mind boggles. My brother-in-law, who regularly reads full-length books and is looked on by several educated people as an authority, tells me that many of these men were in their forties, or more, which is staggering; according to him, the history of Art, currently believed to go back before Christ almost, is teeming with characters who frittered away invaluable production-hours in disgusting leisure-activities such as cutting off their ears, drinking, perverting, going funny in the head, and doing away with themselves. (There was one man with a club foot who took diabolical liberties with his female relatives, believe it or not, and died abroad.) Hardly surprising, then, considering the revolting market-image they presented, that they never

58

managed to get their products across until after they were buried, and the consumers forgot how revolting they were; often, they starved to death with years of potential output still untapped.

You have put your finger(s) right on it, gentlemen, in recognising the need to create artist-incentive; I particularly admired those suggested questions in your handbook which you said you were in a position to answer, such as: *In our works canteen there is a large area which we are thinking of decorating as a mural. We would like some general guidance on prices and specialist artists.* Knowledge that this sort of sensitive, well-heeled market exists will surely stir British artists to creating the kind of paintings, etc., that a decent working-man can take his kids to look at without being ashamed. I also liked Question 2: *I am thinking of buying a modern picture for the boardroom. The budget is £250. Could you advise me on names of suitable artists with an eye to future values?* Your subtle use of punctuation in the last sentence is refreshingly forthright; we all know that no artist worth his salt these days is going to rot in a hovel without main drainage; whether his course is Whitechapel – Tooth's – Shell Mex boardroom; or Stratford East – Haymarket – ITV; or Northern working-class novel – Northern working-class play – Northern working-class film, he is daily demonstrating his concrete approach to realistic idealism in 1964.

I gather that you are not only concerned with getting businessmen to buy pictures, but also that you will be helping struggling artists to find profitable outlets for talent, and this is why I am writing to you. I am a writer, prose mainly, although I have recently opened up a small branch business in occasional verse. I have taken eleven *Write For Profit* courses, whose directors say that with a bit more coaching they will be finished with me, and I have got myself an agent, two lawyers, and an accountant, so I'm ready to go. I have already placed several freelance articles on weddings in our local paper, and am the stand-in woodworm correspondent for the *Pesticide Trade Weekly*. I feel the time is now ripe for me to come out with a best-selling novel, and would be extremely grateful for advice as to what is currently popular with the reading-classes. I visualised something of about four hundred pages of medium-sized print, with a girl on the cover in suspenders, that could be abridged by *Readers' Digest*, and done by the Rank Organisation. (Or M.G.M., but I'm not certain if American supertax is higher than ours.)

Yours in thanks,
Jim Smith.

P.S. – Can you advise me on a suitable pen-name? Beverley something would be nice.

P.P.S. – I understand E.M.I. are giving a 1-for-1 scrip issue. Is it a good time to buy?

April 20th, 1964

Gentlemen:

Many thanks for your help. I have now spent two days in Bethnal Green getting local colour for the Amusing Yiddish Philosopher (played, perhaps, by Meier Tzelniker in the film?), and three days in Chelsea talking to debs, but none of them was pregnant or Communist, so I suppose I'll just have to make that part up. I went to the Elephant yesterday to look for a sympathetic ton-up rebel with a justifiable grudge against society, but some bastards in black jackets threw me down a manhole; however, it didn't turn out too bad, as I was able to get plenty of material on the internal politics of a London hospital for Chapter Four. I'm off to Ladbroke Grove tomorrow to find a melancholy Negro jazzman who can marry the nymphomaniac fashion editor in Chapter Nine, which will finish the first part of the book on a Burning Social Question.

Yours ever,
Fabian Thunder (Mr.)

May 6th.

Gentlemen:

I have now written 40,000 words, and am getting bothered about Income Tax. Is it possible to treat foreign rights as capital gains? Would you suggest 10 per cent gross of the musical version, and could this be spread over ten years, or invested in convertible life insurances by a Swiss bank? I am also planning to fly to Viet Nam for the scene where the transvestite Chinese Communist loses faith with Marx and falls in love with the ex-wife of a director of General Motors, which my agent says will corner the prestige market, and am

60

worried about travel expenses as total deductibles. Also, I have a rather awkward question – am I paying my agent too much? He gets £20 per week, and has moved in upstairs with his cats.

Yours ever,
Fabian Thunder (Ltd.)

May 14th.

Gentlemen:

Viet Nam worked out very well, because the plane came down in the Himalayas with engine-trouble, and while we waited for the rescue teams I was able to knock out two chapters about the cosmic significance of a group of representative people faced with disaster and death. Unfortunately, there were no nuns aboard, but a spaniel went mad, and I did five hundred words for pet-lovers. My broken leg didn't get attention for two days, so I have made my hero a cripple instead of a homosexual, which is just as sympathetic, and more authentic. While I was away, my wife ran off with my agent, and my new agents says there's a chance of getting that bit rewritten by somebody for *Woman's Own*. I wanted to write it myself, but he said I shouldn't burn out my genius on hackwork, and he could probably get £5 for it, which he'd be glad to split with me.

Ever,
Fabian.

P.S. – Are you *certain* it's necessary for an artist to suffer this much?

May 18th.

Gentlemen:

No, I haven't been able to get in any references to Auschwitz yet, but I'm working towards it. My third sub-plot concerns a German who went blind in the First War (I hope to get the book published in time for the fiftieth anniversary), and lived right through everything, which should be O.K. He ends up in a missile project in Cairo, so I can say lots about the Arab Problem and the Bomb, and end the second part of the book on Two Burning Social Questions.

Ever,
Fabian.

Gentlemen:

I have written 100,000 words. Have I finished?

Gratefully yours,

Fabian.

Bye Bye Blackbird,
Hello Mortal Sin

In the days when the keepers of the house shall tremble, and the strong men shall bow themselves, and the grinders cease because they are few, and those that look out of the windows be darkened, I know one boy who won't be sweating. I intend to raise my coffin-lid briskly, throw a few things into an overnight bag, and, whistling something appropriate, prepare to meet my Maker.

Now, don't think I'm complacent about damnation. I know of many a sober pillar of society with adoring kids, unroving eyes, shiny shoes and an impeccable record, who is nevertheless bang in line for the sulphurous pit. There are millions of citizens who wouldn't be caught dead on a primrose path, but who are in for an eternal shock, and when it comes to comparing souls with these paragons, I am just not in their league. Yet I have something up my sleeve – call it a trump card, if your taste runs to honest cliché – which will see me in and out of the Almighty Dock and on the tram to Paradise in double-quick time. I worship innocence.

Not, naturally, the stuff of which virgins, etc., are traditionally compounded. Innocence being stuff which can't exist within the same mortal coil as intelligence, no case can be made out for human beings having any of it. A man is a sack of skin filled with phosphorus and water, liberally garnished with original sin, and that's about the top and bottom of it. Godly men struggle towards the dream of innocence, hoping to get salvation as a prize for a Good Try, and I have nothing but admiration for them. But self-purification is not my long suit; in fact, when it comes to virtue, I hold what looks like an unbeatable misère hand, and it's probably too late for me to do much about it. I prefer to stake my claim to salvation on my efforts to protect innocence where I find it in danger of corruption by Man the Unclean. I shall go down in post-apocalyptic fable as the man who stopped the rot. Or tried to.

Which, of course, brings me to animals. Only in beasts that, as the story goes, want discourse of reason, can we see innocence. Since they lack the capacity to distinguish between right and wrong, this non-faculty gets them off the hook on which humanity swings. If I am one of the sympathetic handful that worships and protects this innocence, others at least recognise it instinctively. When an English cinema audience coldbloodedly watches an air-raid incinerate a town's population, only to fall weeping into the aisles when a dog comes on and moons among the ruins, that groan which shivers the auditorium is no ordinary pitying noise. It is an unconscious recognition of the innocence of a dumb animal imposed on by the chaos created by sinful men. Such an audience is normally excoriated for its callousness, but I'm one of the lads who leads the groaning. After all, what if a village school gets in the way of napalm bomb? The kids would only have grown up into men that leered at women, or women that coveted their neighbour's ox, or something. But to involve a dog in man's evil so that its mute innocence sets off human sin, that's moving. That hurts.

It's hardly necessary to say that it was only a matter of time before human beings began to react to this awareness of the unattainable innocence flaunted in their faces by dogs and goldfish. It's not easy, being the only species of animal condemned to the everlasting bonfire. Which of you, at that awful moment when Lear shrieks out 'Why should a dog, a horse, a rat, have life,/And thou no breath at all?', which of you has not jumped up on your seat and cheered him to the echo?

The first inkling I had that a human plan was afoot to inflict sin on animals in order to take them with us when we go, was the movement in the States to put trousers on dogs. This started as a joke, but within three weeks it had caught on as a serious proposition, and, led by prurient blue-rinsed matrons, it ran like a brushfire across the country, persuading people that nice dogs wore trousers and ones that didn't had dirty minds. Worse – since who cares about people? – this undoubtedly had an effect on the dogs, who were presumably stirred to new depths of lust by the sight of bitches in tantalising fig-leaves. Animal sin was born.

When the movement died, I thought the sin had died with it. I should have had more sense; sin isn't made that way. Once planted, it just hangs around for the propitious moment, and it looks now as though that moment has come. Last week, three newspapers carried three separate items from three separate countries; and they all pointed one way. The first story was a Bavarian idyll concerning Doctor Friedrich Schutz and an enclave of homosexual ducks reared by him on a private pond in the name of, I understand, science. He has raised male mallards who are now irrevocably infatuated with other male mallards, and has even developed an adult duck that can't keep its eyes off geese. However unimpeachable the doctor may claim his motives to be, it can only be a matter of time before one duck in every three is bent and a cataclysmic rot sweeps through freshwater society. Already, psychiatrists throughout the world are jumping up and down with enthusiasm for Dr. Schutz, and no doubt establishing little pockets of perversion in thousands of different ponds. Naturally, the front slogan for their dabblings will be that animals must be sacrificed so that we know more of man, but since man is already lost, the net result of the experiments will simply be to swell the ranks of the damned. Before long, tabloids will be carrying banner headlines announcing ELDERLY DUCK ON SERIOUS CHARGE!, and H.M. Commissioners of Parks will be thrown into the Scrubs for living on immoral earnings. Liberal weeklies will fight for the rights of consenting adult ducks, and then the whole thing will pass into oblivion, carrying with it the irrecoverable innocence of British poultry.

But man's deliberate corruption of animal innocence goes beyond the simplicities of the sexual scene. I have in front of me a tightlipped *Telegraph* clipping which reads:

WASHINGTON, Thursday.
The American Army's latest secret weapon is trained

birds. Just what kind of birds it declines to say. The scheme is wrapped in secrecy.

So. When it comes to bearing the responsibility for the nuclear chopping-block, why should birds get off scot free? Why should man carry the can alone? As if it mattered what kind of bird it was. At least it won't be ducks, who have just become a number one security risk; more likely parrots, or budgies, who will be taught judo and Tonkinese in the Pentagon basement and flown out to Vietnam or Havana, to perch in enemy trees and scream 'Yanqui Si, Cuba NO' or 'G-O-L-D-W-A-T-E-R . . . GOLDWATER!' until some frantic local shies a rock at them and precipitates a World War III in which Western politicians will be able to claim total innocence.

And yet, if I compare these two vile stories with the third, they at least take care to conceal the deeper truths behind the elaborate façades. The third story holds no brief for subtlety; apparently eager to accept the turn things are taking, it gives them a swift kick on their way. It's a report of one of the sideshows in the psychiatrists' hootenanny held in London last week, a piece of straight talking from Dr. Ross V. Speck, in comparison with whom Schutz of Bavaria begins to look like Doctor Doolittle. Speck claimed that pets played a large part in his 'dealings with psychotic families', and that the death or illness of a pet often helped to avert a disaster within the family. 'I recommend a family to buy a pet,' said Speck. 'The situation in some families is very dangerous, and it is better that the animal should die rather than a member of the family.' I'd be hard put to elaborate on the image conjured up by this nauseous gobbet of medical advice. As far as I can make out, Speck is insisting that every household have a small menagerie on tap to act as a sort of clearing-house for the family's neuroses, so that if your wife leaves the top off the toothpaste, you can work off your temper by hurling a few cats out of the window or crucifying a handy newt. After all, why should man's inhumanity be confined to man, when the pet-shops are stocked with cannon-fodder? It's just too bad if the animal you pick on happens to be a sexually-maladjusted duck from one of Dr. Schutz's broken homes, who never had a chance, or a shell-shocked parrot just back from his national service in Hanoi.

One thing's certain. You won't find me fouling up the chances of my immortal soul by spreading sin among our dumb friends. And don't write me off as a sentimental fool too good for this world, either. There are still a few of us left, and I have a *Guardian* paragraph to prove it:

GRANT TO KEEP MOTH HABITAT

The Sussex naturalists' trust has been promised a grant of £250 from the World Wildlife Fund towards the cost of leasing and maintaining the only known habitat in Britain of the Lewes Wave moth. During the past year, members of the trust's conservation corps have cleared scrub that threatened to spoil a breeding site near Lewes.

It's comforting to know that somebody still cares.

A Fine Day
for Miracles

In the meanest little room in the meanest little street in a particularly mean part of our mean metropolis, a kindly old doctor raised his honest, careworn eyes from a rat-bitten orange-crate, and said, gently:

'It is my professional opinion that unless you find, at a rough estimate, ten thousand pounds by, say, Christmas Day, little baby Eric Wormwood, your only child, is liable to depart this life abruptly, due to an Unknown Wasting Disease.'

At this, Mrs. Sadie Wormwood wrung her withered teen-age hands, stifled a sob, pushed a wisp of chromium-blonde wig out of her dropsical eyes, red-rimmed from lack of money, and bit her trembling lip. She had feared the worst, and it had duly materialised; she recognised the Unknown Wasting Disease of old – had not trusty Bette Davis succumbed to it, Joan Crawford, Ronald Colman, Jennifer Jones, Edward Everett Horton, and Champion the Wonder Horse, to name but a few? She knew exactly how it would strike – baby Eric would be waiting, perhaps, at Kennedy International Airport, or similar, when a strange, techni-color dizziness would fuzz his eyes; at first, he would shrug it off. Then some time later he would find he could no longer play the viola. He would drop his knitting, fall down the steps of St. Peter's, lose his balance in a polo match, get beaten five lengths at Longchamps, and, slowly, to a Dmitri Tiomkin score and the full-blown noses of a million matrons, he would peg out with the last rose of summer, or, in his case, Christmas.

'Is there nothing you can do to save our only child on whom our every hope and dream is pinned, following his mother's major internal operation which shall be nameless, but which nevertheless means tiny Eric is destined to pass his life unsiblinged?' cried honest, thin Bill Wormwood, 43, an unemployed Dalston plate-layer.

'Nothing,' said the doctor, gravely. 'All is now with God (from Whom, as luck would have it, all blessings flow), unless you can raise ten thousand leaves of negotiable lettuce, in used notes, please, with which to send little Eric to a warmer climate. You have until Christmas Day, and that will be three guineas because this is officially my afternoon off, and I have better things to do than poke my old fingers down your brat's revolting throat to no profitable purpose.'

With a sigh (the first, it turned out, of many), middle-aged Bill Wormwood smashed the ornamental pig in which he had been keeping the money gained by selling his Dear Old Dad's priceless Military Medal, and handed it to the doctor, who vanished without another word.

As soon as the door fell off behind the elderly gentleman, Bill placed an undernourished arm, encrusted with pitiable wens, about his wife's frail shoulders, and drew her down beside him on their plank.

'Have no fear, my love,' he said softly, 'the good Lord will provide, or I'm a Dutchman, and by Christmas little Eric will be running and jumping and laughing, just like all those lousy little blacks that infest this stinking neighbourhood and make it a place no Christian man would be caught dead in.'

'But *how*, William, whom I love and worship above a number of things? We have but little chance on the despicable pittance (which, incidentally is fit pay for an idiot like you) of raking together the requisite boodle in the next fortnight.'

Forty-three-year-old Bill sprang up suddenly, as a wave of December optimism coursed through his negligible body, and danced a little jig on what was left of the floorboards.

'It is, according to the latest estimates, the season of good-will, cheer, and, above all, miracles. As Dickens, that distiller of nauseous joy, has, or rather had, it: *something will turn up!*'

'All right for some,' muttered Sadie, pulling a dedicated rat from her mildewed cardigan, 'Dickens was coining a bomb.'

'So shall I!' cried Bill, making their one remaining rafter ring seasonably. 'I will have one last desperate, and in its way rather noble, go at selling my plans for the inexpensive construction of a heavier-than-air machine. I will beg, rob banks, steal hubcaps, ply my body for hire in the fortunately vicious streets of our fair city, or get a job.'

His unlovely wife sighed.

'In the meantime,' she said, 'go out and sell the garbage. We have nothing to eat but a few rusks, long past their prime.'

'Put the mice on a low light,' cried Bill. 'I shall be back within the hour, rich beyond the dreams of Hammersmith.'

So saying, he gathered up the week's rubbish in an old, yet faithful, carrier-bag, and hied him to the Portobello Road. As he entered his dealer's shop, Fabian du Cane leapt towards him from a clump of Art Nouveau polystyrene holly, his face a savage mask.

Bill Wormwood reeled back in terror, clutching for support at a priceless roll of Post-Impressionist lino, but Fabian whipped the thing off and handed it to him.

'Nicest bit of savage mask this side of Bayswater,' he said, his lilting Devon brogue inaudible beneath his disgusting Cockney voice. 'Christmas special. Got a man, small way of business, mind, knocks 'em up over a garage in Chingford, nice little wife, four kids, wooden leg but I'm not prejudiced, new Ford Anglia, works at Standard Telephones. Long drag every day from Chingford to Arnos Grove, but that's what it's like these days, 'n'it? Dab hand at the old Melanesian reproductions, this chap. Can't sell enough of 'em. That's the line you oughter be in, that or Polynesian plastics. That's where the money is, believe me. How's the unemployment business?'

'Thriving,' said Bill. 'That's why I'm here. I got some more of them *objets trouvés* I thought you might be interested in.'

'Ah. So happens a boatload of Matrons For Goldwater from Iowa, on their way to convalesce in Samarkand, has e'en this very hour dropped anchor in the Estuary. I've had my man down there since it arrived, handing out brochures and free paper sacks, so I don't doubt they'll be here any minute, ripe for the old gnarled wood mobiles and dried cod charm-bracelets. Let's have a shufty at your gear, quick.'

Wormwood emptied the contents of his bag, and du Cane hurled himself upon them, chuckling the chuckle of the just.

'Lessee – two genuine Portuguese roll-top snuffboxes (you left a bit of sardine in that one, Wormwood, that'll never do) – a late Victorian ball-cock, eminently restorable – six original French corks – an early Edwardian kettle with much of the fur still intact, good, *good* – a Royal child's boot, *excellent!*'

Honest Bill Wormwood shuffled through the heap of rejects.

'Can't you do nothing with this matchless bacon rind?' he said.

'Not at Christmas, mate. Can't shift it. Elk-gut ain't seasonal, see? Trouble with Christmas is it ain't commercial enough, if you get my meaning.'

'What about these Heinz mistletoe containers, then? Or the H.P. long-stem vase, specially designed to hold Christmas roses?'

'Not a chance. Market's flooded. Tell you what, though – that Maxwell House venetian glass tankard might be a seller. Whip the label off, there's a good lad.'

As he removed the label, Wormwood's weary eyes fell on the magic word BINGO! emblazoned across it. He looked closer. He turned it over. On the back was a grid of numbers.

'Here,' he said, in his own inimitable way, 'what's this?'

Du Cane peered over his shoulder.

'Ah. Well, you fill in your name and address and follow the instructions in order to win a free Sunshine Holiday or 10,699 other marvellous prizes.'

Bill Wormwood staggered, grasped the friend's seersucker kimono.

'Would I be right in assuming that the said Sunshine Holiday takes place in a warmer climate? The sort of area that spells dead trouble for Unknown Wasting Diseases?'

'Beyond a doubt,' said du Cane, burnishing a length of gutter.

'A miracle!' cried Wormwood. 'And seasonal, too!' He whipped a wax crayon from his battledress pocket, scribbled on the label, placed it in an envelope, and, pausing only to gabble a short, yet unmistakable prayer, he tugged du Cane's sleeve.

'I need a stamp,' he murmured, 'so how about forking out for the bric-à-brac?'

'Of course,' said the dealer. He made some rapid calculations on the left breast of a washable rubber Venus. 'It comes to exactly threepence.'

'By Heaven!' shouted Wormwood. 'That's precisely what I need. It is clearly my day. You wouldn't, by the remotest chance, have a stamp about you?'

'My last,' said du Cane. 'But seeing as you're a professional colleague, I can let you have it at cost.'

'Bless you!' said Wormwood, through his tears, punching the Queen's face on to the envelope with forgivable zeal.

'Not at all,' said the dealer. 'I like the way you do business. Happy Christmas.'

'Happy Christmas!' shouted Wormwood, and he leapt from the miraculous premises, galloped to the nearest letter-box, and thrust his salvation inside it.

Beside himself at his good fortune (a rare enough occurrence among men of his upbringing and taste), he decided to treat himself to a spin around the smiling heart of our dear pre-Christmas capital. On weightless feet, he sped up Bayswater Road, skirting the now famous Hyde Park, and plunged into the tinsel holocaust of Oxford Street. Above his rejoicing head, plastic angels cavorted, cardboard reindeer leapt from pillar to post, papier-maché bells clanged noiselessly, giant wooden dwarfs beckoned and nodded, and all around the coruscating neons spelled out the universal message:

PEA ON ARTH GOO WILL TO ALL ME

Bill Wormwood moved among the milling, roaring, spending crowds, caught in a fever of bargain-priced happiness, breathless with the contagious joy. He forgot the knife-edged drizzle and looked upon the whirling world through a gentle curtain of Crosbyan snow, trembling with delicious faith. Suddenly, he found himself being swept along in a warm wave of cheering, slavering women, their little fat hands bright with green notes; with his feet clear of the ground, he was carried into Horridge's enormous department store, where he washed up against the perfume counter. Young voluptuaries with omelette-coloured faces and lush green lips sprayed his evil rags with free scent. In fact, everything seemed free; largesse exploded on either hand, and prices tumbled all around him. It was possible, he saw, to buy twisted orange paper, filled with plastic silent whistles and wise saws, for mere pounds; special Christmas carrier-bags were being given away with all purchases over fifty pounds (and everyone seemed to have benefited from the offer, he noticed); whenever a lady bought ten Christmas trees, she was given a free box of candles, and a whole squad of Father Christmasses were on hand to give advice and promises to kiddies for no more than the price of an electric train-set. Without paying a penny, he was allowed to watch the demonstration of a machine for extracting juice from carrots, and to listen to the Garden Furniture Department Chorus sing his favourite carols. All around, benevolent floorwalkers were giving away free handbills that must have cost a fortune to produce. At last, his pockets stuffed with valuable glossy paper, Bill Wormwood, intoxicated with the spirit of giving and the warm contact of his fellow-beings, waltzed out into the teeming street, and went happily home.

Back once more among the familiar meanness, he rushed across the door of his hovel, snatched his wife from the shelf, and covered her with the kisses of a plate-layer inflamed.

'Baby Eric is saved!' he cried.

Sadie Wormwood picked up her wig from the floor, spat into it cautiously, and stuck it back on.

'By what means?' she asked.

'By a miracle, of course!' snapped her husband, 'from the Portobello Road, as it happens!'

She stared at him, plummy eyes glazed with suspicion.

'How much did you get for the junk?'

'What is mere money,' cried Wormwood, 'compared with miracles?'

His wife groaned, and smote the festering wall.

'You didn't let that bent bastard fob you off with yet another packet of beans which will be thrown out of the window and not grow into a plant capable of reaching Heaven, but instead die of frost like last Tuesday?'

'No.'

'Another goose that not only refuses to lay golden eggs,

73

but is also rotten with fowl pest and unfit for human consumption?'

'None of these, my love. I exchanged the trash for a Sunshine Holiday.'

'In a warmer climate?'

'The very same.'

'Show me!'

'I didn't actually bring it with me. But I've ordered it.'

'Dearest!' cried Sadie, dropping her knotty hands from his throat. 'You just sit there and I'll put the kettle on, and we'll have a nice cup of hot water. By the way,' she added, 'I suppose we won't need it now, but I've written off to Littlewood's for £200,000 in return for 1d., as advertised.'

'My dove!' murmured Wormwood, 'my own Christmas angel. We shall now be able to buy some shoes, sandwiches, and reading matter, etc., for the journey. Not that I like the idea of my little wife working, but every bit helps.'

So it was, then, that on the following Saturday, while baby Eric gurgled optimistically in his crate, the Wormwoods sat down together with their ears pressed to the wall, the copy coupon between them, and listened to the football results on their neighbour's radio. At the end of the broadcast, they smiled at one another with an expression of the non-surprise that generally goes with faith.

'To think we ever doubted!' cooed Sadie. 'We have the requisite eight draws, just as I planned, no more, no less.'

'God bless us, every one!' cried Wormwood.

The rest of the story is part of the imperishable heritage of fairytale. There were forty-seven draws that week, and the first dividend was 1½d. A man in Huddersfield won the Sunshine Holiday, and the other 10,699 gifts were scattered the length and breadth of the land, none of them lengthily nor broadly enough to reach the Wormwood household. On Christmas Day, just as the first bells pealed, little Eric, true to form as ever, Wasted Away and was buried in a pauper's grave. But nevertheless, twenty million citizens throughout the queendom were happier than they had ever been on a Christmas Day before. This was only half the population, but it was an extremely high average, and one can't, after all, expect miracles.

The Rich
Get Richer
and the Poor
Get Ulcers

Last week's news item concerning the man who stole to keep from starving because his wife blew all his wages on bingo must have pizzicatoed a lot of heartstrings; and if, like me, you sympathise with the poor woman driven to bingo by a hubbie so lacking in imagination as to cough up all his sweated coin into her maniacal fingers, then there is good news yet to hear and fine things to be seen, before we go to Carey Street by way of Sweet Sixteen. Happiness is just a thing called *Competitors Journal and Money Matters*.

This succulent gobbet of yellowpress schweinerei was delivered to my desk last week, free of its sixpenny charge. Why, I can't think, unless it's because I pass its Fleet Street offices twice a day; it's on the cards that the editor keeps a squad of highly-trained pauper-spotters stationed round the clock at a window overlooking the street; when someone like me shuffles past in a khaki gas-cape and second-hand surgical boots, a complex organisation swings into play which by sundown has programmed a rundown on the victim's overdraft, unpaid bills, frustrated ambitions, and inherent gullibility. The next day, *Competitors Journal* turns up in the morning mail, and another generation of wage-packets is bound for death or glory.

This newspaper, for all its tarty title, is actually a sort of *Which?* report on grabbing. Coming into its inheritance in the age of the green stamp, the betting shot, the bingoleum, the free offer, the Something-For-Nothing Era, *Competitors Journal* is a ragbag anthology of competitions culled from newspapers, trade-ads, come-ons, and the like, which offer everything from holidays in Spain to a lifetime of free moth-balls. The editorial ethic seems to be: It's not the principle, it's the money; the pages are dedicated to encouraging fifty people to cast their daily bread upon the waters on the off-chance that one of them may end up with cake. It carries the features of a regular daily, but all these are angled towards eliciting the money-making potential of the area involved. Nothing, apparently, need be done for fun; un-profitable leisure is a mug's game. It's impossible to separate ads. from copy, especially when it comes to the advice-mongers, some of whom are on the staff, some freelance marketers of heads-I-win-tails-you-lose offers, who are the only people who can hope to get an income out of the com-petitions. For example, Billy Snape claims that, for a mere twenty-five per cent of your winnings, he will put you among the 'latest successes in OMO; OSRAM; SHIP MATCHES; BISTO; TANGO; BRYLCREEM; JOHNSON'S WAX; NESTLE'S; CROSSE AND BLACKWELL'S; DANISH BACON, etc.' Even if Mr. Snape is capable of picking winners, the more people who benefit through him, the smaller their cut of the prize cake. And Billy's income not only remains the same as far as commission goes, he also makes on his tips at six bob per selection, and enters the contests free of either charge or risk. The paper provides a platform for dozens like him, and since most of the contests require labels, boxtops and evidence of purchase, the *Journal*'s existence must make a lot of admen and sales managers sleep more easily. Be nice if one could say the same for the competitors.

These pitches are the direct approach, of course; but there's subtler stuff, too. In case you thought that flowers were designed to some other end than profit, the horticul-tural column, 'Growing Cash', will soon clear up that little misconception. And their survey of the arts doesn't leave much to be desired, since desire is its aesthetic canon. Sup-pose you're in love, engaged, that sort of thing – stymied for a way of making it work for you? You obviously haven't been following T. W. Newland, your genial radio critic, who has dug up a Radio Luxembourg contest where all you have to do is be officially engaged and tell a hilarious anecdote about your courtship. Happy listeners will bust a gut laugh-ing at your romance, and you may well wind up with a 21-

piece tea set. Also on the current broadcasting page is a snap of Ludwig Koch, sitting in a meadow with earphones on his head, smiling in a way that only naturalists can these days. Since no news has reached you of Ludwig's having pulled off the jackpot in the Maggi Soup Contest, you read on, only to discover that the B.B.C.'s up to the same game now, with a competition called 'Wild Life on Tape', where the best recording nets twenty-five guineas. Of course, this is a deal of cognoscenti only, and any pater-familias *au fait* with the facts of modern life will be sweating blood over the Crosse and Blackwell's Costa Brava Holiday coupon; but it's quite possible that the layman can pick up matchless recordings of earwigs mating from Billy Snape or one of his confrères, and win from behind. Hottest news on the radio page is the *Top of the Form* is to go for broke: 'First, there's a trophy to be won – an overdue innovation,' says the paper. They're dead right you know; it's no life being a kid, coming home to your peeling hovel at four p.m. to find your emaciated parents struggling feebly over a five bob bingo win. A kid could get maladjusted that way. Which is why the paper has a Children's Page, too, to start the tinies off right. That's the way to redress social imbalances. Give a kid to *Competitors Journal* until he's seven years old, and he'll be theirs forever.

Social abuses, actually, are a regular concern of this rag. Correction of injustice lies through improvement of competition facilities. Their current leader propagandises for a Pensioners' Football Pool: 'Give the old 'uns a real chance of getting among the divvies . . . ' The great thing about a three quid pension is that it could buy you seven hundred lines of Treble Chance, isn't it?

Not that the paper misses out on important news. On page 14 this week, there's a notice of a discussion to be held at the London Competitors' Club (the headline reads, by the way, 'L.C.C. MEETING') on the current Nescafé contest, and there's news, too, of this year's National Lambing Competitions, not to mention a photograph on the front page of The Most Glamorous Grandmother in Britain, who's there only because she pulled down £1,000 for her efforts, and a write-up of the winner of the Kellogg's All Bran Contest.

Oh, it's not that one objects to gambling, or even to a

system of opportunities that enable a man literally to go to the dogs; a human being still has choice, and it's a little late in the day to impose a censorship on it. What is really objectionable is this sort of secondary capitalisation upon weakness, this direction of aim towards life, leisure and the pursuit of free washing-machines, and this adulation of Charlie Nobody who's just raked in a thousand pounds for listing the virtues of a scouring-powder. And gambling is somehow less offensive because of the general anonymity of the competition; one's resentment of bookies, or the tote, or the house-odds isn't as great as one's jealousy of the identifiable couple in the next street who've spotted the ball and paid off the mortgage. We have enough encouragements to envy and greed in the affluent society, as it is; cupidity's imbalance can do without the jolly predictions on this paper's horoscope page 'THIS WEEK'S BIRTHDAYS: The Stars give you every encouragement – MONEY, PRESTIGE and other worldly advancements: you can't go wrong where these are concerned. But Love, Friendship and the Family need some extra care later in the year.' I'll just bet they do. *Money Matters*, runs the paper's sub-title. Not that much, it doesn't.

Sigmund Freud and
the Jelly Babies

'Wow!' it said. There was a fixed smile on its little face. 'Betcha can hardly wait to sink your teeth into *me!*'

I turned it over, and found a perfectly ordinary piece of ground beef, wrapped in Cellophane. On one side, however, this ur-hamburger bore a recent portrait of itself with little googly eyes, tiny limbs, and a mouth from which the above remark ballooned.

'I'm fatless,' it went on. 'We all are. We're the purest! We're JUMBOBURGERS!!'

New as I was to Californian supermarketeering, I didn't intend to get conned by half a pound of scrag. I held it up.

'You can wipe that smile off your face,' I hissed. 'Good family or no, you are about to be hurled into boiling fat and eaten. That's how we treat mincemeat where I come from.'

The woman next to me turned, a pink giblet trembling between thumb and forefinger. She smiled uneasily.

'Did you say something to me?'

'No,' I said. 'It probably came from that pork chop over there. If it insults you, call the manager and have it thrown out. This is a respectable joint.'

The other shoppers fell back, hurriedly but respectfully, and the Jumboburger and I went to buy some vegetables. The same hysterical anthropomorphism had hit the frozen food section. 'Boyoboyoboy!' shouted the broccoli, little green faces shining up from their frosted cartons, 'Tasty Tendertips for YOU!' One particular pea, whose P.R.O. man was obviously a cut above the rest, maintained that its whole life had been one long ritualistic preparation for the glorious instant of self-immolation in my peptic juices.

Eventually, of course, I grew used to this sort of spiel. I accepted the animated neons of dancing hot-dogs and talking prawns (although one particular hotel-room in downtown Minneapolis, whose window overlooked a chorus line of singing chips, sticks in the memory), but I never quite understood the motivation behind this area of advertising, what prompted the admen to believe in the richness of this particular seam. I'd have thought that the last relationship to be striven for between food and eater was one of friendship and brotherhood. I'm no vegetarian romantic: I know that the lambkin gambolling prettily beside its dam is destined for parsley spats and a hint of mint, but the recognition that today's sonnet is tomorrow's stew is one of the inescapable facts of growing up, and one adjusts to it. However, I don't choose to be constantly reminded of this, or to sit down to a steak that claims to have been martyred rather than grilled.

Nevertheless, I did, as I say, come to accept this as part of the American scene, and was quite content to attribute whatever appeal these advertisements were supposed to have to some unfathomable quirk in Americans. I was therefore particularly disturbed when I returned to England and found that the phenomenon of articulate grub was by now commonplace. Just the other night I happened to catch that commercial for chocolate-covered peanuts, the one where a nubile little nut introduces itself, says: 'I'm a delicious peanut – look what happens to me!' and dives into a pool of liquid chocolate, from which it emerges looking like Al Jolson. It is then embalmed in sugar and shown to melt in the mouth, not in the hand. Luckily, there were no kids around to see this grisly cradle-to-the-grave career, because the effect it had on me was decidedly odd. A corner of the veil had been lifted, briefly; and what I had seen in the half-light was something unimaginably sickening.

Whatever else they may be, admen are no fools when it comes to selling their product. They've compiled their own Psychopathologies of Everyday Life, and have a fair idea of the teeming cesspool that is the average shopper's Id. With the right sort of insinuation, they can sell a convertible to a man who's always considered his marriage to be reasonably successful, and make a cigarette addict of someone who's spent his life believing that a boy's best pal was his mother. So that when they pitch their sales talk at an attempt to humanise slices of bacon and packets of crisps, they're not mistakenly creating a ludicrous relationship between consumer and article. They're playing on something which they can see, even though we may be unaware of it; that Man is basically cannibal.

Allow me a scientific digression, since this is a serious business. Hardy's theory concerning Man's predilection for sea food claims that this is a vestigial characteristic of the period when nothing distinguished the subdenominations of primates except muscle. We and the apes were, as far as the impartial onlooker was concerned, a group of hirsute lumps pottering about the jungle trying to keep body and soul together. But some of the lumps were tougher than others, and when the food ran low, the weaker lumps were driven towards the sea, where many of them perished except those intelligent enough to stand up on their hind legs and thus avoid drowning in shallow water. However, the situation for these lumps was intolerable; here they were with their new-found brains, incapable of feeding themselves and unable to get back to the yams, beetles and other goodies on which the toughs were gorging themselves. They probably stood around for an eon or two before coming up with the idea of hunting for food in the sea. Being intelligent, they had evolved the system of bashing things together, which they then applied to oysters, mussels and so on, and survived. A substantiation of this theory (to which, admittedly, I haven't been able to do full justice) is that the convolutions of hair-formation on the human body manifest signs of primordial water-adaptibility.

Now, to apply this to the chocolate peanut and the dancing chip (are you with me?), we may fairly attribute our taste for humanised delicacies (which the admen have long understood and abused) to the period when the consumption of actual human flesh was not the social blunder it is today. Cannibalism, of course, was not ubiquitous, and the rise of sensitivity put paid to it in the end. But this is an external reason, a white man's accretion; *taste* for human flesh did not necessarily diminish, and less sober tribes have only recently been persuaded to stop dining off one another, proving that there's nothing wrong with the stuff itself, just that one man's meat is another man's uncle, and this is difficult for the Secretary for Commonwealth Relations to condone. The urge to cannibalism has been subsumed – most strikingly, by sexual passion, where terms like 'hunger', 'appetite', 'satiety', and the rest, testify to a ghoulish sublimation of one urge in another. 'Lechery' itself comes from an Old Teutonic word for gluttony, cognate with 'lick'. See?

Armed with this knowledge, the admen have advanced. A sexual slant is all very well for simple things like motorboats and Harris Tweed, but to sell food, they have to go deeper than that, through sex, to the very nub. To cannibalism itself. And if they ever have misgivings about the correctness of the theory, they need only borrow a leaf from Freud's book and observe the eating-habits of children. It is not a pleasant thing to watch a small boy eat a jelly-baby. He usually starts with the head, joyfully, and works horribly down to the toes. I have stood by powerless while three tiny girls dismembered a gingerbread man and gobbled him up, and watched members of my own family lick a sugar-mouse into nothingness, having first named it Charlie (after a blood-relative) and played with it for two hours. Children, obviously, need concrete evidence that their food is surrogate man-flesh; their primitive, basic urges can be satisfied only by chocolate clowns and creamfilled santas and marzipan golliwogs. Maturity brings sophistication; meat doesn't have to be moulded into human shape, but if it talks, dances, attempts to make friends, then the urge to buy, cook and eat becomes irresistible.

I don't pretend this isn't an ugly theory; but it's irrefutable. And one of the nastier aspects of the whole business is that civilisation has a tendency to break out in abreactive rashes; beneath our bland deodorised surfaces, repressed primitivisms jostle and nudge, waiting for their chance. For now, all we can do is rely upon the admen to keep us satisfied with imitations. I hope they can be trusted.

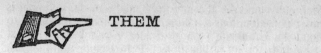 THEM

End as a Man

In the enormous State University where these events took place, the Medical Centre, is, in every respect, the very pulse of the machine. 25,000 students set their bearings by its colossal tower, their routine by its chime, and their careers by its judgments. It is, naturally, the largest building, with the brightest bricks, the newest plumbing, the cleanest windows, the whitest corridors, and the roomiest parking-lots. In these essential features, the School of Business Administration runs it a close second, but any rivalry that thereby exists between them does so on a good-natured level, the members of each faculty being closer to one another than they are to anyone else. This is primarily because they share the same attitudes towards their subjects, and the same aspirations concerning their futures. It is, you see, self-evident to the simplest clod that the only things worth being in life are either a doctor with a businessman's income, or a businessman with a doctor's status. If you can't be a professional footballer, that is.

The University Administration treats medical students and embryo businessmen alike with the sort of respect that used to be shown to men reading Greats at Oxford. Admin doesn't have to worry about *their* orientation and adjustment, since their choice of career demonstrates their obvious intelligence and commonsense. Similarly, all educational principles are brought into line with the Highest Common Factor of these two schools. 'LEARNING' is the name given to an electronically-computed, statistically-controlled, IBM-remembered system of credits and debits out of which eventually emerges the new Magnanimous Man. And the polar considerations for admittance to the University are, first, the candidate's physical and psychological fitness, second, the utility of his subject. Before being admitted, he is depth-probed physically and mentally, injected against disease and investigated against dissent. He is then conveyed to the Administration who will analyse him by computer and convert him into four easy-to-handle IBM cards, on which his individuality will be represented by a pattern of punctures. When the cards of any one class are stacked together and held up to a bright light, little beams should spike out from all the holes. If any hole is blocked, the card is removed and the candidate re-examined more intensively. Now, businessmen and doctors are without exception perfect cards, and are the first to be invited to faculty barbecues. They are also rewarded by the most stimulating conditions for study – rooms of exactly proportioned dimensions, temperatures and colours, with more loudspeakers, more lavatories, more coffee-machines, more TV sets, and more wallspace for hanging up diplomas and snapshots of your brother the surgeon.

Buildings and their amenities deteriorate in relation to Admin's evaluation of the worthiness of the study-subject. At the bottom of the scale is a group of decrepit, permanently disorientated, shifty-eyed pariahs who have a tendency to shuffle away when looked at hard, and to intermarry with disgusting results. These, God help them, are English Literature students, and they may be found huddled in evil-smelling knots around a leprous shack advertised in the handbook as the oldest building on campus. It is thus invested with a spurious dignity, as far as tourists are concerned. But the *real* symbolic value of its sixty-year-old decomposition, its pitiful facilities, its isolation from the scene of any real activity, can't be mistaken. The students there carry forever the stigma that once, when their ancestors' cards were being fed into the electronic paterfamilias, the machine coughed, belched, and fused the lights on the entire campus. At this point, all the doctors phoned all the businessmen, and their two buildings rocked with boyish laughter. The fusing, in fact, was purely coincidental, but, as with all good universities, it's the tradition that counts.

This information is set out for the benefit of those unfamiliar with this system, to underline the fact that my own story is more than just the old one of an ingenu caught in the cogs of any impersonal organisation. It's rather the clash between one English teacher bred in an academic environment which encouraged individuality and one psychiatrist whose responsibility was the creation of a standardised identity. Because, whatever the indignities perpetrated upon the personality of the student, they're nothing to the investigations made into each new member of the staff. Understandably enough – after all, from his potential is to be created the Teaching Norm. Should his students differentiate themselves to the point of deviating from this Norm, then it is the teacher's duty to bring such wanderers back from their private imaginations into the shelter of good, sterile community.

I passed the physical part of my initiation without difficulty, and spent the rest of that day answering the psychiatric questionnaire. Three days later, I was summoned to the psychiatric division on the twentieth floor of the Medical Centre, and shown into a deep-pile waiting-room by a nurse who closed the door with a curious animal laugh. No doubt my treatment of the doorknob had brought the refrain of some half-forgotten Freudian mnemonic to her mind. I was left alone in a large pale-pink dome, where I stood for some time like a fly trapped under a dishcover, until a tall square-headed man in a white coat slid in softly, stared at me with his head on one side, and said, very gently: 'Sit down. Relax. Nobody's going to hurt you.' Then he went out.

I sank into a leather pit that had been prepared for me, and stared at the goldfish tanks, trying to locate the loudspeaker that was murmuring Viennese waltzes; the music seemed to be seeping out of a vase of flowers. I struggled out of the chair, and when the doctor came back, noiselessly, I had my head buried among the plastic roses, and my arms around the pot. With his hand on my shoulder, I froze; I fought to turn my twisted grin into an endearing smile.

'Pretty little things, aren't they?' I said.

He laid a hand on my arm, which I realised was still around the belly of the vase.

'Why don't we let go of our pot now?' he said. 'Then we can go inside and have a chat.'

I walked into the office in his shadow. He closed the door, and when he moved away I could see five young men watching me, all with their heads bent in exactly the same way as his. All wore identical white coats, carried black pencils in their left hands, black notebooks in their right. Psychiatry students.

'Gentlemen,' said the doctor, 'this is Mr. Coren. You remember his card?'

They all wrote down 'This is Mr Coren', and nodded, remembering my card. This was the processed form of the questionnaire I'd answered, known as the M.P.I., or Multiphasic Personality Inventory, which consisted of two hundred almost unanswerable questions allowing only the reply YES or NO. This fact is extremely important, given alternatives like:

'I like my father better than my mother' (a) Yes.

(b) No.

or:

'I would rather be marooned on a desert island with:

(a) My mother.

(b) My best male friend.

I sat down, to find that my chair was six inches lower than anyone else's and was so constructed as to render all movement impossible, except for an occasional desperate flutter of either hand. All I could see of the doctor was his eyes above the desk rim.

'Let's see,' he said. 'You're from Europe, right?'

'England,' I said. Politely.

He glared at me.

'That's what I said. You have socialised medicine there, don't you?'

I smiled.

'I suppose you could call it that.'

'*We* do,' he said. A strange throaty mumbling issued from the five students. 'Well now, Mr. Coren, we've examined your M.P.I. with considerable interest. Yep – that's what we examined it with.'

I tried to shift in my seat, aware for the first time that I was pinned down by the only ray of sunlight coming into the room. I dug my heels in the carpet, pushing, but the chair wouldn't budge. The doctor was staring at me.

'Mr. Peterson – would you be good enough to help him, please?'

The student dragged me out of the sunlight.

'Thank you,' I said. 'I must be out of condition.'

The doctor closed one eye.

'Never really *were* what you might call a sporting type, were you?'

'Not wholly.'

He waggled my cards at me, and I stared at them malevolently.

'Says here you don't like playing football, only watching it. That right?'

'Yes, that's right.'

'Find it exciting to watch?'

'Yes,' I said, 'don't you?'

He smiled, looking down.

'All depends what you mean by *exciting.*'

The students creaked in their chairs.

'Most of what we need to know is down here. Just a coupla little things I'd like to clear up, though. Straighten out – so there's no misunderstanding, know what I mean?'

I nodded, for form's sake. The backs of my knees were wet.

'Now, this question 67. How about filling out a little?' he frowned when I couldn't remember, then said through his teeth: 'The desert island.'

'Oh. Yes.'

'Well, from cross-referencing your answer-codes, and correlating your tendency-ratings, it looked to us as though you were maybe trying to hide something here.' He leaned forward, lowered his voice: 'Would you *really* like to spend the rest of your life alone with your mother?'

'Of course not! Come to that, I wouldn't want . . . '

He shut me up with a raised ballpoint.

'Felt kinda – guilty – about admitting you preferred the company of a man to that of a woman close to you, is that it?'

'That's ridiculous,' I said. 'It's not a woman, it's my mother!'

There was dead silence for a second; it broke on the scratching of five pencils. I watched the dust turn gently in the solitary sunbeam.

'Well – let's leave that, shall we? I'd like to check this one you left blank. The Rorschach.'

'All I could see was inkblots,' I said. 'They didn't look like anything else.'

He sat back, smiling, and I couldn't see anything but his hair.

'Funny that. This is strictly between ourselves, but did you know that eighty-seven per cent of our examinees said that the blots reminded them of women?'

I smiled, relaxing.

'That's comforting,' I said. 'At least you can see I don't have an unhealthy preoccupation with women, can't you?'

He blew his nose, and punched it back and forth with the rolled handkerchief, not answering. Suddenly, he said:

'Still writing poetry?'

'As a matter of fact, yes.'

'Kinda gets a hold on you after a bit, doesn't it?'

'Oh, you feel that too?'

They all stared at me, motionless.

'Look,' said the doctor at last, 'as a faculty member, you had the option to live in private lodgings, didn't you? I mean, you weren't *forced* to live in a dormitory with three hundred male graduates, were you?'

'It's the only address the University gave me. Besides, I didn't like the idea of an obligation to someone else's home and family, you know?'

'Idea of a family make you sort of – uncomfortable?'

'No – well – yes, I suppose it does in a way. You see . . . '

He leaned forward, chinning his hands.

'Go to a segregated school?'

'All white, if that's what you mean.'

He sighed.

'All *male* is what I mean, my friend.'

'There was a matron . . . ' I said weakly.

'Beatings?'

I started to define corporal punishment, but he was looking at the students.

'Must've been tough on a poet who didn't like football.'

'Look,' I said, 'I liked football then, and anyway, I had friends, close friends.'

The students scribbled frenziedly. The doctor cracked his knuckles.

'What's this about ballet? You list it here as a Main Interest, under section 19. That so?'

'I like it sometimes.'

'Get stimulated by it, would you say?'

'I don't know what word I'd use. How do you react to it?'

He examined the tip of his ballpoint, minutely.

'Don't have much ballet around here. Guess the Russians don't stop by the same way they do in London. Pretty popular over there, aren't they?'

The students had stopped writing. A fly thrashed itself to death against the window.

'Actually,' I said, through my teeth, 'I always vote Conservative.'

'Hold on there!' said the doctor, '*Admit* to voting Socialist if it'll make you feel any better. We don't give a good goddam how you vote. Not our business. We're only here to help you.'

'That's nice of you.'

There was a pause.

'Why *do* you?' said the doctor.

'Why do I what?'

'Vote Red.'

'If you must know,' I said, 'it's because the British Labour Party stands for the adoption of the thumbscrew, state maintenance of homosexuals, secession of the South, euthanasia for all mothers over forty, capital punishment for professional footballers, and the increased population of Red China. That's why I vote for them.'

The doctor looked across at the students.

'He had to have a reason for saying all that, didn't he, Hackenschmidt?'

'Indisputably, sir.'

'Thank you, Hackenschmidt.'

'Thank *you*, sir.'

The doctor stood up, glinting at his henchmen, who shot to their feet like synchronised flick-knives. I couldn't quite make it out of the chair, and sat in the middle of the white circle.

'I'd like to have you come back next Tuesday, same time,' said the doctor. 'So's we can have a little chat about things.'

'What things?'

The sun was in my eyes again, so that I couldn't distinguish his face. The large silhouette said:

'Oh – you know – ' it jabbed at its ear with a thick finger ' – things.'

I managed to get out of the chair. Hackenschmidt had stepped forward to help me, but had obviously thought better of it, and had got back into line.

'I'm not sure I'll have time,' I said.

The doctor opened the door for me.

'It'd be wisest if you found it,' he said.

Up until then, I'd been rooming with a quiet, pleasant, middle-aged political scientist from Denver. We didn't talk much, but we both smoked, took the occasional beer together, and listened to the same sort of gramophone records. We got on pretty well, all in all. Two days after my interview, I was re-accommodated in a single room, next door to the warden of the dormitory. He showed it to me personally.

'Didn't realise we still had a single one left,' he said, uncomfortably.

'Funny, that,' I said, 'seeing that it's next door to yours.'

He tried to laugh.

'Never know what's going on right under your nose,' he said. There was an ugly pause, during which his laugh withered, and he looked away. 'You'll be better off here, though.'

A man came past, slid between us with a muttered 'Excuse me,' took his name-plate off my new door, looked at me, hard, and walked away again.

I didn't see much of the warden after that. Come to think of it, I didn't see much of anybody.

Ah, Did You Once See
Shelley Plain?

'I don't believe it,' said Guardi, who teaches Freshman Italian. He had been struck down with hiccups immediately after dinner, and was trying to drink his coffee from the wrong side of the cup.

I turned off the radio.

'Why not Malraux?' asked Hoffmann.

'Moravia,' said Guardi, sadly. He hiccupped, and blew coffee over an exam-paper he was marking. 'Moravia, if anybody.' He wiped an elbow over the paper, and failed the candidate. 'But then – there is nobody, really.'

A melancholy settled on the room. I was sorry I hadn't turned the radio off earlier, after the announcement of the blockade of Cuba and the invasion of India. That would have been all right. But news which makes college teachers unhappy is that which serves to substantiate their belief that genius goes ever unrewarded, and the givers-of-rings are blind.

'But after all,' I said brightly, 'Does anyone take the Nobel Prize seriously?'

They did not hear.

'Nobody – ' said Karnapp, who has been working on his doctoral dissertation for fourteen years, and has buried three good professors and five little magazines, ' – can persuade me that Steinbeck is anybody but a third-rate hack literary opportunist.'

Nobody tried.

'Fifth-rate,' said Karnapp. He glared at us belligerently.

'Doesn't he live near here?' I said.

'Seventeen thousand dollars,' said Hoffman quietly. 'And you get to make a speech.'

'Swedes,' said Guardi viciously. He tore an essay in half and wiped his pen.

'Salinas,' said Karnapp. 'He lives in Salinas. Ten miles from Castroville. The Artichoke Capital Of The World.'

He laughed diabolically, and left.

'I might run down there,' I said. 'If there's a chance to talk to him. Or to find out what the people think about him. After all, he's supposed to be a Great American Writer.'

'Of and for the People,' said Guardi thickly. Everyone laughed miserably.

'Exactly,' I said.

They all stood up to go. At the door, Hoffmann turned, looked at me pityingly, and shrugged.

'It's your life,' he said. 'If you want to go, go.' He waited for the others to pass into the corridor, took out a piece of paper and scribbled a number on it. 'First phone this guy in San Francisco. He'll help you.' He pushed the paper into my hand. 'Don't mention this to anyone.' He turned up his coat-collar, and was gone.

I dialled the number. It rang for some time. Then two women and a jazz-band answered.

'I hope you'll excuse me . . . ' I began.

'Who?'

'What did he say?'

'Is Willi Holst there?' I shouted.

'It's Joe!'

'JOE! We was all just talking about ya . . . '

'I'm afraid you're mistaken, madame,' I said. 'Wesley Hoffmann gave me your . . . '

'Whyn't ya call earlier, Joe? Whereya been?'

' . . . number, and I . . . '

'Haveta speak up, Joe, we got the Hi-Fi turned on full.'

'We been going out of our *mind*, Joe. They said you had a hernia.'

'They said you wouldn't be able to dance no more.'

'IS WILLI THERE?' I screamed.

'Sure. He's on top of the escritoire.'

'Boarding up the windows. He says there's gonna be an air-raid. They invaded India, Joe, didja hear?'

There was a crash, then silence.

'Jesus!' moaned one of the women. 'He fell on the goddam Hi-Fi.'

A man's voice on the phone.

'Four hunnerd bucks, Joe. Three months' work.'

'I'm not Joe.'

A pause.

'Who are ya?'

'A friend of Wesley Hoffmann's. I called about Steinbeck.'

'You bastard,' said Willi quietly. 'You lousy bastard. I coulda still been on top of the escritoire. Three months to get the speakers facing right. Had to knock down two walls.'

'I'm sorry. I just wanted to know how to contact Steinbeck.'

'John Steinbeck?'

'Yes. The Great American Writer.'

The laughter of the three died down.

'I'm sorry,' said Willi choking. 'Here's whatya do. Go to Monterey, look up George Ober. Gotta pencil?'

Monterey is the first town on the Strip, fifty miles south of San Francisco. The Strip extends to San Luis Obispo, or, at least, it did last week. It grows longer all the time, and its present two hundred miles may suddenly stretch to accommodate a new influx of artists. On one side lies the Pacific, on the other the Santa Lucia hills. It is as far West as the world can go, and thousands of Americans have come here, to hesitate like uncertain lemmings between the mountains and the sea, because there is nowhere else for them to go, because civilisation seems further away than it is, and because Artists (as opposed to artists) are the most gregarious people in the world. And so, in green declivities in the red hills, dozens of tiny communities have sprung up, believing in their own self-containment, painting pictures of one another and selling them to one another, trading rope-sandals for sunglasses, and writing savage indictments of America. In longhand.

Ober lived in one of these canyons, a few miles south of Monterey. As I drove, the sea-fog came up and folded me in, and I became aware of a beadstring of yellow foglamps in the mirror, tailing me along El Camino Real, slowing when I slowed, accelerating when I did, finally stopping when I stopped, beside a sign that said 'Partington Canyon'. I got out, to check on the narrow road that scuttled away into the canyon on my left. The driver of the car behind, a station-wagon loaded with easels and children, wound down his window.

'Is it here?' he shouted.

'Is what here?'

'The Community.'

'No,' I said. 'It's further on. You can't miss it. They're all out front painting.'

The car bucked in first gear, and spun away at breakneck speed into the fog. Three others raced after it, followed by a pick-up truck carrying a huge block of marble. I heard the tyres scream around a distant bend.

Half-way up the canyon road, I swung off into the fore-court of a large ramshackle house, just visible through the fog, and through great heaps of driftwood and junk. I pulled in and heard the groan of cheap metal giving away to rock. I got out resignedly. The front wing was buckled; crunched against a towering stone monolith, a few flakes of paint waited for me to notice them, then detached themselves and floated down. The door of the house opened, and a dim figure came running through the heaps; he turned out to be a tall thin blonde man in a violet kimono.

'Excuse me . . . ' I said.

He was staring past me at the car. Or, rather, the rock.

'You've destroyed my Venus,' he moaned.

I looked at the eight-foot rock and the buckled wing.

'I'd say Venus came out on top.'

He stooped and picked up a microscopic fragment of rock.

'Desecrated!' He glowered at me. 'I pulled her from the sea, and she was perfect. She came in the night, and when the tide went out, she was standing there, on the Pacific beach. I had been waiting a long time for her.' He took hold of my arm and shook it, waving his other hand towards the agglomerations of flotsam. 'We were all waiting.' He let go of my sleeve with a shudder. 'You think painting driftwood and selling it to philistines like you is my life? This was my sea-garden. I made this Paradise. It was innocent. And now it is tainted.'

'I'm sorry,' I said pleasantly, trying not to look as though I'd just slithered down a tree-trunk with a pippin and a leer, 'I was looking for George Ober. He's supposed to live here.'

'Ober?' He laughed nastily. 'They took Ober away last month. He blew his stack. Didn't you hear?'

'No.'

'Yeah. He had the studio upstairs. He used to be a restaurant signwriter. He was the greatest signwriter in the world, he said. Only it wasn't Art, know what I mean? So he came here and started painting. Only everything looked like hamburgers. He used to go down to the beach and come back with rocks. And they all looked like hamburgers. So he went to bed for a month. When he got up he was smiling. He started painting again. He came rushing in to me one morning, screaming. 'Look!' he said, 'I finally made it. An abstract.' He showed me this painting. 'What does it do to you?' he shouted. I looked at it. 'It's a hot-dog,' I said. Three days later, the highway patrol brought him in. They'd found him on the beach. He'd just carved the biggest minute steak in the world and was trying to slash his wrists with the chisel.'

'Damn!' I said. 'He was going to tell me about Steinbeck.'

'Who's Steinbeck?'

'He's a Great American Writer.'

'Yeah? Like Ober was a Great American Painter?'

'That hadn't occurred to me,' I said.

'Best thing you can do is drive back to Monterey. There's a bar there Ober used to hang about in. The Warehouse. On Cannery Row. Maybe this Steinway hangs out there too.'

So. Cannery Row. The fantastic cunning primitives of Steinbeck came back into my mind, running between the boilers, scrapping for life down on the Row, the beach-combing princes and the bum philosophers, the frog-hunters and the moonshiners. And the Row was still there. I drove fast into Monterey.

It wasn't hard to find Cannery Row. It was pretty well sign-posted. I turned down from the clean sunbright main street towards the waterfront, peering left and right, antici-pating deterioration, looking for drunks in the gutters and poetry scrawled on the walls. If anything, the houses im-proved, the smell was clean salt, the streets were wide and full of young women pushing new prams. And then, abruptly, there was Cannery Row. And one sardine cannery. I pulled into its car-park.

'Clean for a cannery,' I said to the attendant.

'Yeah. Don't do much business now, either. Keep it that way for the tourists.'

'Tourists?'

'That's right. Never did figure out why they came. Good restaurants, I guess. Or else some politico musta died here or got born or something.'

I walked back down the Row. Clean, white. Three art-shoppes with different coloured awnings; two of them displaying driftwood, one an exhibition of pictures of seaweed, and fishermen with pipes and tiny mis-shapen hands. A sandal-maker's, where a woman with wedding-cake earrings was dusting the bullfight posters. The Steinbeck Theatre (Peter Sellars in 'Waltz of the Toreadors'), The Steinbeck Boutique. A dress-shop hung with cardboard chinoiserie, yclept 'Cannery Row Originals'. Strollers in Jaeger casuals and hand-made sandals. Two long, low, obviously expensive restaurants loaded down with enamel decorations from grateful diners' clubs, and an all-glass bar built on an artificial promontory over the sea. No boilers. No shacks. No drunks. No stench. Just a slight smell of tasteful disinfectant overlaying the offensive sea-weed. A stage-set for a travel-poster.

The Warehouse lay back from the Row. Perhaps it really had been a warehouse once. But I was beginning to doubt whether anything here had been anything once, if you know what I mean. A man peered through a slit, asked me if Joe had sent me, laughed, and let me in. Inside, a huge vault, the brick walls painted bright red to simulate brick walls, the concrete ceiling painted grey to simulate a concrete ceiling. Dozens of tables painted like roulette-cloths. A dais, where a negro in eyeshield and shoulder-holster played 'You Called Me Baby Doll A Year Ago' on an upright piano. Theatre-bills of the nineties pasted on the William Morris walls; looked at closely, they turned out to be reproductions of theatre-bills. Good ones, though. Cracks painted in the windows, and in the long mirror behind the bar. I sat down, and a waitress in rhinestones and a red-silk tasselled dress shimmied up. She's going to ask me to Charleston, I thought miserably.

'I'll have a beer,' I said.

Two well-dressed portly people, man and wife, sat at the next table, talking to an Artist. Beside them, they had propped what could only have been a fair cut of the young man's stock. The top one was of a flight of seagulls that should have been made in porcelain and nailed to a boarding-house wall.

'I don't profess to know anything about art,' the man was saying, 'but don't I trace an influence of Winslow Homer in your work?'

'Or Norman Rockwell, maybe?' said his wife.

The young man blushed.

When the waitress came back, I asked her if John Steinbeck ever came in.

'What's he look like?'

'He has a moustache, and . . .'

'They all got moustaches this year. Last year was beards.'

'He did "The Grapes Of Wrath",' I said helpfully.

'You're wrong,' she said. 'I saw that. That was Henry Fonda.'

'No, you don't quite follow,' I said. ' "Of Mice And Men" was his, too.'

'Uh-uh.' She shook her head. 'That was Lon Chaney. And Burgess Meredith. Wasn't nobody had a moustache in that.'

I finished my beer. The piano-player struck out desperately with 'Darktown Strutters' Ball', and a few people started singing. The waitress came back.

'I just remembered. There was this little guy with a moustache name was John something in "For Whom The Bell Tolls". Not Gary Cooper, the other one. Maybe that was him.'

'No,' I said. I picked up my bill. 'No, that was Ernest Hemingway.'

7

It Tolls for Thee

Manhattan's largest fallout shelter, the New York Telephone Company Building rising near the Hudson River, will have 21 storeys without a single window. The vertically striped fortress will house 3,000 workers, who will be capable of surviving a near-miss atomic attack for two weeks.

Life Magazine, November 9th, 1962

For the first few moments, I was convinced that some joker had directed me to the sanctum sanctorum of one of California's more esoteric sects. The doors sighed shut, sealing me into a huge pastel-coloured hall; on the facing wall was etched the outline of a bell, beneath which stood a long low table flanked by two gently revolving plastic bushes hung with pink, blue, olive and yellow telephones. A row of multi-coloured phones, doubtless freshly picked, garnished the table. Behind these sat a motionless young woman, smiling fixedly. In order to approach her, it was necessary to pass between two long rows of identical desks, on each side of which stood a telephone of a different colour, and a rack of pamphlets. No one sat at the desks, and, apart from myself and the votary at the far end of the hall, the place was empty. It is almost impossible to walk down a long aisle towards someone who has been trained to smile. I committed the miserable error of starting my own smile as I began to walk; consequently, by the time I reached the table, I had considerable difficulty in speaking through the grinning death-mask into which my face had been turned.

'Good morning,' I gritted. 'I should like to have a telephone installed in my apartment.'

'Yes, sir,' she murmured, softly. 'If you'll wait over there by the lavender instrument, I'll have someone help you with your problem.'

'I haven't got a problem,' I said. 'I want a phone. Can't I just leave my name and address with you?'

'I'm sorry, sir.' The same monotone coming through the glazed smile. 'Bell Telephone has found that the most efficient way of dealing with clients' problems is through the instrument.'

I sat at the desk, looking at the Instrument, wondering whether I ought to smile at it. I heard the girl murmuring on her own telephone. I casually opened one of the bright pamphlets in front of me, and found the familiar catechismal layout prescribed by P.R. departments of the great industrial organisms. I turned the pages with waiting-room languor, impervious by now to the frenetic hyperbole; after all, I had known before coming here that the nett worth of Bell Telephone approximates to that of England, that it is wealthier than the five wealthiest states in the Union, that soon it will have a satellite all to itself, and so on. I was beyond surprise by Bell. And then, on the last page of the pamphlet, I came on this: 'At present there are more than 85 million phones in the U.S., and by 1975 there will be more than 160 million.' I went back and re-read it. And realised that the telephone was reproducing at approximately three times the rate of the population of China. This in itself, all other implications aside, had a staggering effect on me. Until then, I had, like almost everyone else, accepted as the two yardsticks by which all other quantities were to be measured, the distance to the Moon, and the population of China. (I have never needed any others, since, at fourteen, I spent two weeks in bed on glucose following a maths master's attempts to conceptualise infinity for me. We cornered it at one point, and had it belittled to the ignominy of one-over-nothing. I thought about this for a few moments; then I cracked.) Told that: 'The 1962 model was driven 250,000 miles on two quarts of oil and one tyre-change. This is the distance from here to the Moon,' I am happy. Or that: 'In 1961, we manufactured one billion ballbearings, or enough to give every man, woman, and child in China

99

two ballbearings each', I know where I stand. Or knew. Not any longer. Now that small fund of conversation-stopping statistics that I have hoarded for bad moments at parties will have to be completely revised in terms of telephones, lengths of cable, warehouse-loads of dials. I shall have to teach my sons that every fifth child born is destined to become a telephonist. Stuff like that.

The Instrument cut through this morbid reverie. A voice of metallic silk introduced itself, and elicited a file-ful of irrelevant personal information before asking, finally:

'Now, sir, how large is the apartment?'

'Three rooms,' I said.

'So you should be able to get along with only one extension. Is that to be a wall-phone, or a Princess Bedside?'

'I want one instrument,' I said. 'With a long cord.'

A metal snigger.

'Oh, come, sir! Nobody has long cords any more. Our researchers found that so many accidents were caused by cords getting tangled up with children and pets and things of that nature.'

'I haven't got anything of that nature,' I said.

'Well, at least you'll need a Home Interphone. So that you can communicate with the party in the other rooms.'

'There aren't any parties. I live alone.'

'Don't you ever have guests?'

Of course, since she lived at the end of a lavender cable, the idea that people actually indulged in the gross obscenity of talking face to face could hardly be insisted upon by me.

'No,' I said meekly, 'No guests.'

A pause. I could see the inside of her brain visualising a banner headline: 'ONE-PHONE RECLUSE FOUND STRANGLED BY ANTIQUE CORD. BODY DISCOVERED AFTER THREE WEEKS BY JANITOR.' I wanted to meet her, I wanted her to see that I was healthy, that there was a spring in my step, that I smiled. But this was impossible.

'Oh, well,' said the voice. 'Of course, you can never tell when a party may drop by.' I wondered whether she was human enough to be trying to console me. The voice sighed, and went on: 'Well then, sir, perhaps we can decide on the colour of the Instrument.'

'Black.'

A tin gasp.

'Beige, green, grey, yellow, white, pink, blue, turquoise!'
A pause. 'Nobody has black, sir. We couldn't guarantee a
new Instrument in black. What is the colour-scheme of your
room?'

In fact, it's pale-green. But I knew the consequences of
my admitting this. So I joked. I thought.

'It's black,' I said. 'Black wallpaper, black ceiling, black
fitted carpet. Black furniture.' I waited for her laugh.

'We-e-ell,' she said, 'Why not have a white Instrument to
set it off?'

'All right,' I said running my tongue over my lips. 'All
right, white.'

'Wish I could persuade you to have a coloured Instrument. Everyone else does, you know. They're so much more
individual.'

'Yes. Well, that's all, I suppose?'

'But we haven't decided on the chime yet, have we?'

'The what?'

'The chime. You can have a conventional ring if you
choose, but for the Discerning we are now able to offer a
Gentle, Cheerful Chime Adjustable To Suit Your Activities
Or Your Mood.'

'But how do I know what mood I'll be in when it chimes?'

'But on some days, don't you just *long* for a Gentle
Chime?'

I closed my eyes. For three weeks I have carried on a
running fight with my landlord over my request to change
my door-chime for a buzzer. And two weeks ago I bought,
or, rather, was sold, a Discount House Bargain which keeps
perfect time all day, and, having been set for nine a.m.,
awakes me up at 4.17 by chiming crazily and hurling scald-
ing coffee over the walls and carpet.

'No, dear,' I said wearily, 'I'm something of a strident
buzz man myself.'

'As you choose, sir.' I could hear her hesitate. I knew she
was cracking. Finally she murmured: 'The Princess Bedside
lights up at night.'

'Quite possibly,' I said, and replaced the receiver.

After I left the building, I stopped to buy the copy of
Life from which I quoted at the beginning of this story. And
suddenly I saw her, and her sad sorority, in their last hours,

101

in their windowless concrete pillar above the rubble of New York. Three thousand telephonists, connected only by a web of lavender cable, frantically dialling and re-dialling, while the nightlights flash, and the bells chime gently, over a dead world.

Requiem for a Nympholept

Valour and Innocence
Have latterly gone hence
To certain death by certain shame attended.
Kipling

(*Reno, Nevada. A broom-cupboard with twin beds, in the attic of the Hotel X. Enter severally a bellboy and two unsavoury Englishmen, Coren and Wiggins. The bellboy switches on a flyblown overhead bulb, and waits, smiling. C. and W. stare at him for some minutes. Finally, the bellboy switches off the light, and exit.*)

Wiggins (*turns on light*): A snip at forty bucks.

Coren (*gloomily*): God knows why we came in the first place.

W. (*opens shabby suitcase, takes out toothbrush and dartboard, and puts in a Gideon Bible, a china shepherdess, two ashtrays, and a shaving-towel*): We are here upon the wilder shores of love, Coren, to mark, learn, and inwardly digest, thereafter to go home secure in the knowledge that bachelorhood is the swaddling-cloth of sanity. The local industry being an interlocking complex of divorce, remarriage, promiscuity and gambling, there is, consequently, an Atmosphere. The air will be good for you.

C.: Wiggins, I am sick of your feeble attempts to drag me into loneliness in order to shore up your cynicism. I am in love, Wiggins, and soon am to be welded in holy whatnot to the Girl Of My Dreams till death us do part. Pipe,

103

slippers, a joint bank-account, and breakfast-laughter are destined to be mine. I am unshakable.

W. (*unscrews bathroom mirror and lays it carefully in case*): Singula de nobis anni praedantur euntes. Thirty per cent of American marriages end in divorce. The rate rises daily. Many of them end, and start, here. It takes six weeks to get unshackled, but only fifteen minutes to couple. Give a hand – (*W. and C. roll up the bathmat*) – we are, *sans doute*, the only one-eyed men in this hotel of the blind. The three hundred others are in the limbo of inter-maritality. Waiting for freedom. And – God help them – most of them spend their six weeks in dodging aspirant mates from the jetsam of the opposite sex.

C. (*takes out picture of Beloved and smiles secretly*): Love is not love which alters when it alteration finds. I intend to play a little discreet poker, and occupy my mind with thoughts of shoes, rice and tax-relief.

W. (*removes pillowcases*): Nonsense! We shall, gay bachelors that we are, and recognising that forty-six per cent of said divorces occur between the ages of twenty and thirty, stroll among the carnage in search of easy pickings for the evening's sport. The Incurable Romantic, Coren, has not yet been born.

(*Alarums off. Sennet without.*)

W.: Aha! Le five o'clock! Shall we join the divorcées?

(*Exeunt hurriedly. Outside the elevator a middle-aged man lies expiring in a pool of martini and blood, a hatpin through his shirtfront. Wiggins drags Coren into the lift. They descend.*)

SCENE II

(*The main bar and lounge. Since there has been time for only one or two highballs, there is as yet little disorder. Large bands of bejewelled predatory women circulate in the half-light, but other than an occasional grab at an individual who has somehow been separated from the groups of shifty-eyed muttering men lurking defensively in the plush corners, there is no open contact. Several décolletées matrons crouch by the lift-gates, watching the arrow descend the scale. It stops. They tense. The door opens.*)

Wiggins: Of course, you have to be able to handle ...

(*Six fat arms plunge into the lift and take hold of Wiggins, who is dragged out screaming. Coren hastily closes door, and ascends. The braceleted arm stuck in the door disappears as the lift passes the third floor. Coren stops lift, leaves it, and makes his way circumspectly down the staircase. At the final bend, he is in time to see Wiggins, clad only in cellular underwear, being hauled into the Ladies' Bar by his I. Zingari tie. Coren sprints down the remaining stairs and across the hall, side-stepping several howling bacchanti, but it is too late. It is the last he sees of Wiggins. Warned by a rattle of rhinestones, he dodges a huge silken female bearing down on him, and vaults an overturned sofa. Beneath it cowers another man.*)*

Man: Who are you?

C.: A guest.

M. (*peers at C. suspiciously*): Not one of my damned children, are you?

C.: Decidedly not.

M.: Thought you might be, with that crummy suit, and all. She's always doing this to me. Trying to screw me on alimony. Sends my kids around looking like they was war-orphans.

(*A podgy hand, bright with rings, grasps the edge of the sofa. The man bites it fiercely. The hand disappears.*)

M.: Worse'n usual this evening. You down here for the six weeks.

C.: No. Just overnight.

M. (*laughs delightedly*): Got away from the wife, huh, huh?

C.: Not married. (*The man bursts into tears, so Coren hastily draws snapshot of Beloved from wallet, and flourishes it. The man backs into his corner of the dugout, trembling.*) Shall be soon, though.

(*The man, hearing this, licks his lips, and looks round nervously, but there is nowhere to go. He smiles sickly.*)

M.: Ha-ha-ha! Now, you just wait there, fellah. It'll be okay. Don't get excited. Rest is the best thing, believe me. I ain't gonna hurtcha.

C. (*heatedly*): You're treating me as if I'm crazy, or something!
   (*Man hesitates, nods.*) Look, chum, I happen to be in love, and . . .

(*The man screams, stifles it, and scrambles out of the shelter.*

He makes an open run for the Men's Room, but is cut down by a hail of maraschino cherries, and dragged away. By this time, several gangs are engaged in vicious in-fighting. After a moment, another man dives behind the sofa. He is stripped to the waist, and across his chest, written in lipstick, is: 'JULIE'S'.)

Man *(breathless)*: Nearly had me! Didja know they got a goddamned chapel in this hotel? Sure – resident judge, whole deal. Takes fifteen minutes. They throw in two roses, hunk of wedding cake, an old boot, and four Polaroid pictures of the happy couple. All for twenty-five bills.

C. *(snorts derisively)*: Nobody can make you marry!

M. *(sneers)*: No? She just says you're nervous, is all. She slips the witnesses a coupla fins, glomps a big smile on the judge, and that's it. Don't tell *me* – I had four weeks of this. *(Angrily.)* What the hell kind of a State *is* this? They told me you could get divorced easy. But I gotta be here six weeks to prove residence. I'll never make it. *(Offers hand.)* Joe Follett.

(They shake. A military band off. The fighting ceases abruptly, and the combatants rush together to the windows. Coren and Follett join the cheering crowd. Coming down the street, following the band to the blast of 'Colonel Bogie', is a column of young men in blazers. Girls dance beside them, scattering them with rose-petals.)

C.: What's all that, for God's sake?

F. *(sighs)*: They're co-respondents. They're marching down to the airport to meet the evening flight from Los Angeles. Gotta hand it to 'em, whatever you normally feel about civil servants. These boys do a great job.

(The manager takes advantage of the momentary lull to announce the first floorshow of the evening. After the overture and Dance of the Eunuchs, which delights the audience to such an extent that several eight-year-olds, brought along as material witnesses, elope quietly, Coren and Follett escape to the bar. A small man is crying into his whiskey. F. pats his shoulder sympathetically.)

F.: What's the trouble, old buddy?

Man *(sobs)*: My wife understands me.

F. *(winces)*: Tough break!

(The little man blows his nose, slips off the bar-stool, walks out of the hotel, and throws himself under a bus.)

F. (*reflectively*): Really, when you think about it, divorce is a beautiful thing. I mean, it's probably the one true moral action in which any two people ever indulge. (*Waves aside C.'s protest.*) A cool, careful, adult decision to preserve their sanity and personalities. Jesus! – a bit different from marriage, huh? When you think that the average marrying age for women is twenty, and men, twenty-two. I mean, what are they? Kids! 'S'getting younger every day, too. But a good thing, that – see, I reckon things'll be helluva lot better when a hunnerd per cent of marriages end in divorce. I mean, how the hell can you commit yourself to a death-do-us-part deal when you don't even know the meaning of the words? Want my opinion, I figure it's only people who've been divorced can ever get married with an even chance of the thing holding water.

C. (*croaks*): Love . . .

F. (*stares at him, snarls*): What're ya, some kind of – a Romantic, or something? Yeah – betcha one of the card-carrying Romantics, huh? Betcha gotta picture in your wallet of some dollie . . .

(*Coren looks away quickly, and watches cabaret. Two red-nosed comedians held the spotlight. One is dressed in ballet-skirt and pigtails.*)

1st Com.: *When* are you coming to live at home, Daddy?

2nd Com.: Never, sweetheart. (*Cheers from the audience.*)

1st Com.: Will I have to get a new daddy? (*Male cries of 'NO!' 'The hell with it!' Sporadic scuffling breaks out.*)

2nd Com.: I'm your Daddy, and you're my baby, and nothing will ever change that. (*Roar of laughter from audience; comedians execute series of pratfalls and funny walks, and exeunt.*)

Follett: See, I been there three times, buddy, so I oughter know the old score, right? I'm getting better every time.

C.: You can't tell me there's no such thing as a perfect love-match.

F. (*chokes*): Urrgh! (*Recovers.*) Yeah, sure there is. There's also pearls in oysters, the Irish Sweep, and a chance for every red-blooded American kid to get to be President. So do not despair, young friend.

(*At this very moment, a Happy Couple appear at the desk and ask for the honeymoon suite as it is their Golden Wed-*

ding. The manager reels back in horror, snaps his fingers, and four bouncers appear. The couple are savagely put asunder.)

C. (*triumphantly*): You see, Follett! As flies to wanton boys
    are we to the System . . .

(*The cabaret over, the fighting has broken out with renewed savagery. Follett snatches the declaiming Coren from the claws of the fleshy vanguard, and carries him to the Men's Room.*)

SCENE III

(*A large ornate lavatory, packed with men in shirtsleeves. Some are bathing their wounds; some playing poker despondently; some, resigned to their fate, are bent over a washstand, tending a small fire of money, chequebooks, and credit cards. A thin man stands on a lavatory-seat, trying to whip the crowd into some spirit of resistance, with no success. Suddenly, he stops, a finger to his lips; a hush falls. Silence within the bunker, and without.*)

Man: I don't like it. It's too quiet.

(*A roar of sound breaks from the Musak system. We hear Sinatra singing: 'Love is lovelier/The second time around.' A terrified clamour rises from the assembled men.*)

C.: What is it?

F. (*darkly*): They've got the transmitter.

(*The men become sullenly silent. The poker-players, who have paused, shrug, look at one another, and pass the cards to the man on the seat. Silently, he elbows through the crowd; each man takes a card. There is thunderous banging at the door, and shrill, unintelligible shrieking. Coren picks a card. It is the Ace of Spades.*)

C.: Now what?

F.: Tough luck, old buddy. You're first man over the
    top.

C.: This is nonsense! I won't go! They'll tear me apart!

F. (*sneering*): Ya lousy Romantic! (*A gasp from the men. Cries of 'Rommie!' 'Romsymp!' One of the men steps forward and sticks a white feather in C.'s lapel.*)

F. (*softening*): Come on, kid, luck of the draw. This comes
    to all of us sometime. It's all over in fifteen minutes. Just
    say 'I do' – it'll make it easier on you.

(Coren backs towards a cubicle, but before he can insert a dime, hands are laid on him, and he is dragged to the door.)

C. *(screaming)*: But I don't love them! *(Shouts of derision, catcalls.)* NO! NO! This isn't the way! THIS IS NOT THE WAY IT HAS TO BE!

(The bolt is slid back. At the last moment, determined to fall as he has lived, Coren prepares to shout the name of the Beloved. But in the panic, he cannot remember. The door opens. There is a momentary glimpse of red slavering mouths and groping fingers and greedy eyes, before

THE CURTAIN FALLS

Gentlemen v. Players

The hill-climbing power of a Cushman Champion Electric lets you take steep hills straight up where other cars must travel on the bias. Add to the time-proven, trouble-free engineering, the fine modern styling of the Cushman, and you see why this is the most popular golf car on the course today.

The Fort Knox Putter – Made of 14-carat gold, designed by a leading jeweler, $200 to $1,000. Hess Bros., Allentown, Pa.

Hooch Handle – Fine golf umbrella has a special handle that unscrews to reveal flask.

Esquire advertisements

The parking-attendant at the third tee waved the four golf-cars into line; the drivers drew up, and switched off. Above them, a faint blue petrol-haze hung in the still air.

'Jesus!' said Hummer. 'What a day! What heat!'

'Yeah,' said Sorfik, in the car beside him. 'Howja manage to stay alive innat goddam beancan? Whyncha get with the crowd and pick up one of these open jobs?'

Belt, in the third car, leaned forward and turned off his radio.

'They ain't so hot,' he said. 'Comes a sudden shower, where's ya protection? A guy could catch pneumonia.' He flicked a switch, and a small plastic hood snapped over his car. The others could see him inside, smiling.

Fender's caddy jumped out, and ran round to open his master's door. Fender strolled across to his partners. He ran a finger along Belt's coachwork, and shouted through the plastic top.

'TIN! It's all tin, Belt!' He waved at his own car. 'Steel chassis, Italian styling, real imitation pigskin seats, automatic transmo, air-conditioner. Imported. Whatsa guy in your position doing inna bug-trap like this?'

Belt got out sheepishly.

'Din't know they was on the market. This month's *Esquire* didn't get here yet.'

The four players walked six yards to the tee, mopping their faces. Hummer looked at Sorfik approvingly.

'*Those*,' he said, 'I like. The mohair plus fours. Style!'

'I gottan anorak to match,' said Sorfik excitedly. 'Hold on, fellas, this ya haveta see!' He ran back to his car.

'Not my taste at all,' said Fender, quietly, to Belt. 'Flashy. Me, I like a good Harris Tweed outfit. Imported.' He showed Belt the label.

'Nice,' said Belt. 'But it's ninety inna shade. Aintcha uncomfortable?'

Fender screwed up his face, and sweatdrops scuttled down the new wrinkles. 'What's this "uncomfortable" jazz? I'm playing *golf*, fella, or didja forget? Suppose I meet someone onna links, a business competitor, or something – you want me to look like a tramp?'

He selected an alligator-handled driver and sent his ball sixty yards down the fairway; his caddy ran up, and brushed the fragments of divot from Fender's coat.

'Gotta good boy there,' said Sorfik.

'The best,' said Fender fiercely. 'Scotch. Imported. Say something, Angus.'

'It's a braw, bricht, moonlicht nicht, tonicht,' said the caddy.

'Fantastic!' cried Hummer. 'The genuine article.'

'I've always had coloureds,' said Belt, grudgingly. 'You know where you are with coloureds.'

He swung his club, cut a black swathe in the turf, and knocked the ball a dozen yards away.

'Goddam balls cost a buck apiece,' muttered Belt. 'You'd think they could turn out a decent ball for a buck.'

Fender looked at him stonily. 'Without a sealskin inner shell, you're nothing,' he said. 'Buck eighty-five.'

The three drove off noisily in their cars, leaving Belt to

try again. This time, his ball went a clear seventy yards. He ran happily to his car, leapt in, and roared off.

'What kepcha?' asked Fender. 'Me and the boys was talking about holidays.'

'I just got back from Palm Springs,' said Hummer proudly. 'Nine courses. Swimming pools. Nightclubs. Jet from L.A. takes forty minutes.'

'It took me two hours in the helicopter,' said Belt. 'But it's cosier.'

Sorfik was making a casual study of his lizardskin golf-shoes.

'You all gotta come round some night, see the movie I shot at the Royal and Ancient,' he said. They were silent, so he glanced up. 'It's a European golf-course. I got colour-slides, too.'

'Where did *you* go?' said Belt, to Fender.

'Capri.' Hummer and Belt looked respectful. Sorfik hesitated.

'Good links?' he asked levelly.

'Private,' snapped Fender. 'Ordinary tourists don't get to play. I got these Wop business associates. With a chateau.'

Sorfik slashed at his ball; it sliced away from him, bounced off a tree, hit the roof of a passing golf-car, and rolled into a bunker. Silently, he changed into Grecian sandals, and drove away. They watched him vanish into the pit.

'A bad loser,' said Hummer.

'Yeah,' said Fender. 'Some sportsman!'

They teed up, and got sixty yards nearer the green; Belt wiped his brow ostentatiously, and cried: 'Waddya say to a drink, fellas?'

Before they could reply, he had unscrewed the handle of his golf umbrella and withdrawn a flask. He offered them plastic containers shaped like golfballs.

'Pretty cute, huh? Here, take some bourbon.'

Hummer unscrewed his own umbrella. 'I prefer Scotch.'

Chastened, Belt turned to Fender, only to find him watching his caddy decant the liquor from two golf-umbrellas into the shaft of a fake Number Three iron. Fender sipped.

'Too much vermouth,' he said. 'And ya bruised the gin.'

Since all that could be seen of Sorfik was a small sand-storm gathered around an astrakhan deerstalker, the three

112

went off without him. However, a few yards short of the green they lost Hummer, when a party of four women in a D.A.R. Golfibus ignored a 'Halt – Fairway Ahead' sign, and rammed him. Fender and Belt did not wait for the ambulance. There was little anyone could do for Hummer.

'Should have had a steel chassis,' said Fender, selecting a putter. The caddy handed him his Fort Knox Putter, and giving the shot plenty of wrist, so that the gold faces glinted in the sun, he hammered the ball past the hole, and off the green.

Belt took his Klondike 18-carat Special, and sank the putt. Fender glowered at him.

'I guess that diamond thumb-mark really helps,' said Belt amicably.

'Lemme see!' Fender whipped an eye-glass from its doe-skin pouch, squinted at Belt's club, and threw it down triumphantly.

'I thought so!' he cried. 'A rhinestone! They fooled ya.'

Belt set his jaw.

'Those sons-of-bitches!' He lowered his voice. 'You won't let this get out, old buddy?'

'Rely on me,' said Fender. 'Except I don't see how I can give you the hole.'

Belt rubbed the golden club against his chin, frowning.

'I guess you're right,' he said. 'My lousy luck. Still – you can't win 'em all.'

'Don't take it bad,' said Fender, marking his card. 'It's all in the game.'

8

No, But I Saw the Movie

Up until a very short time ago, no nation on earth enjoyed as splendid a popular Image in the United States as the English; the visiting Briton basked. And no one ever asked him actually to demonstrate those qualities on which his glory was based; he was simply required to Be. Whatever his personal appearance, whatever his character, or behaviour, or background, when he passed through a crowded room, hushes fell, beautiful women gnawed their lower lip, strong men dropped their eyes, and small boys lifted their shining faces, as to the sun. For all knew this man's inheritance. Not, necessarily, the facts of it; but this ignorance was unimportant to them. Across a thousand panoramic screens, they had seen his clouds of glory trailed, and now, encountering the Englishman in the flesh, they recognised the presence of something greater than they knew. And so they roared at jokes they did not understand, because the English Sense of Humour was a rare and precious thing, they nodded at his truisms, seeing immediately their hoary wisdom, they saw his inarticulacy as noble taciturnity amid the sounding brass; and husbands, noticing their wives' idolatrous looks, dashed in herds to their tailors to order suits made up from old army blankets, specifying the dashing trousers, flared at the knee, the cunningly asymmetrical jacket, the skilfully frayed shirtcuffs.

Americans, in that sweet not-so-long syne, knew where respect was due. Millions of feet of celluloid had taught it them, and they had met nothing to say it was not so. They had seen the Englishmen in War, whistling dirty songs at the

114

Japanese, escaping in guffawing droves from cretinous camp-commandants, knocking back bitter in the mess before going out with a boyish toss of the head to paste Jerry over Kent, while all the world wondered. Americans had gaped at the Miniver set, picking shrapnel out of their tea and fussing over the Young Conservatives' Picnic. In Peace, too, they had seen and doted; England was God's Little Acre, a thatch-dotted paradise of trafficless lanes where blithe spirits in veteran cars chugged from one hunt ball to another, swam in Piper-Heidsieck, watched the dawn come up over Pont Street, and spent their serious hours redecorating mews cottages. Just as Jack Hawkins had been everybody's C.O., so now everybody's Daddy was Cecil Parker, and Basil Radford and Naunton Wayne were always running through the drawing-room on the way to Ascot. Between War and Peace, there were Times Of Stress, when the British, played by John Mills disguised as Richard Todd, or vice versa, tightened their belts, stiffened their lips, chased the natives out of the rubber, and went back to their airmail copies of the *Telegraph*. The Common Folk, of course, were a splendid bunch. In War, they died uncomplainingly like flies, sat in the ruins of their homes and told uproarious Cockney stories, and, adrift in a lifeboat with Noel Coward, were never at a loss for a spirited song. When Peace came, they all went back to being chauffeurs, bus-conductors, publicans, comic burglars, bank clerks, and Stanley Holloway. They were deliriously happy.

When I first came to America, this image still hadn't changed much. True, a backward glance from New York towards the horizon might have caught those little fistshaped clouds forming, but it was some time before the first cans of Truth were unloaded on the docks. At first, it was easy to argue my way out of American suspicion. *Look Back In Anger? Room At The Top?* Flashes in the pan, I said. I would laugh nervously. Alarmist minorities, I said. But when the new wave of British filmmaking broke across this continent and swamped Old Albion in its scummy tide, I knew I was beaten. For, worst of all, it hit at a time when some of the facts of English life were finally filtering through to the average American; word was out that the garlands were showing a tendency to wither on the brow, and the films provided the clincher. America knows. Over the last few months, San Francisco cinemas have shown: *Saturday Night And Sunday Morning, The Entertainer, A Taste Of Honey, The Long And The Short And The Tall, Sons And Lovers, The Loneliness Of The Longdistance Runner, Term Of Trial* and *A Kind Of Loving*. In succession; to packed houses; and against the background of *Time*'s articles on the decline of Britain, and Mr Acheson's penetrating twang.

Now, I'm not complaining. I'm delighted, Lord knows, that English filmmen are at last making films. I can hold up my head among the cognoscenti. But not among the masses. And this overnight switch of Image is hard to bear. Now these Americans who once looked on me with awe, look with derision, or pity, or revulsion. If they bother to look at all. For they know the Truth. They know that I was born in a narrow street, in a scrofulous terraced hovel, to a withered old mother of twenty-four, her delivery screams drowned by the roar of the machine-shop/pit disaster. As a child, I stumbled wretchedly about in a pall of silicotic filth, unaware of the sun, occasionally catching a dim glimpse of my father, an emaciated creature in long underwear and a cloth cap, as he was dragged home, stewed to the gills on dole-money, from the local thieves' kitchen. I never had much of an education, due to long absences from my hellish school after regular beatings by me mum's fancy-man (tattersall waistcoat, moustache, Vauxhall), and week-end jaunts to drizzleswept boarding-houses with the nubile milk-monitor in 5A. However, the educational problem was easily solved by sending me: (a) to Borstal, where I was thrashed by the staff, humiliated by Etonians, and ostracised by my fellows, or (b) to a bicycle factory where I got my kicks from dropping dead rats (with which England is bubonically overrun) into the packed lunches, or (c) – if I was a girl – down to the waterfront to watch the boats. A short time later, sex reared the ugliest head outside a Hammer Film; due to the constant presence of drunks in underwear mashing tea all over the hovel, I pursued love's young dream in bus-shelters, grimy cinemas, on canal-banks, behind billboards, and so on. My partners in the great awakening were diverse; every American schoolboy knows that I have: (a) Gone to bed with the foreman's wife and got her pregnant, (b) Gone to bed with the blonde from the typists' pool and got her pregnant, (c) Gone to bed with one of the sailors and got myself pregnant. This is the new Time Of Stress, and acting in the new True British Fashion, I faced the problem squarely by: (a) Nipping off to my auntie, the cheery abortionist, (b) Marrying the girl and promising her a life of loveless squalor, (c) Playing house with a young homosexual and waiting for the Day.

But suppose I managed to survive this *jeunesse dorée*; what then? Well, I might have gone into showbiz, and, living the glamorous life of a matinée idol in Bootle summer stock, entered my senior years without (from sheer luck) having got anyone pregnant, and with the comfy recognition that I was merely an alcoholic failure. Alternatively, had I gone into a respectable profession like teaching, I would have got all the plums the other fellows got (penury, frustration, domestic disaster, social rejection) simply by giving private lessons to a little girl to keep myself from the workhouse. Naturally, there was justice in all this – if I hadn't been a dirty pacifist, and had gone off to Burma to whistle with the rest of the lads, I could have landed a job in a public school. Mind you, I mightn't have got a look-in on the whistling routine; the Americans now know that I should have wound up in a grass hut with six typical British chaps, beating the living hell out of a senile Japanese until his mates turned up to square the odds and give us what we deserved.

Nevertheless, though I have been passing these last months with all the misery of an ad-man watching the Truth knock the stuffing out of a beloved Image, it wasn't until last night that I actually broke and ran. The cinema that had been responsible for most of the punishment suddenly interrupted its run of English films to show an American low-budget movie, called *David And Lisa*, and since this took as its subject two young inmates of a mental hospital, I went along with glee at the prospect of having the ball in my court for a rare hour or so. The manager smiled at me in the lobby.

'Hi there!' he said. 'Just in time for the short subject. You'll like it. It's an English documentary.'

'Splendid!' I said, with a touch of the old panache. After all, I was safe enough. It was probably a Pathé Pictorial, one of those delightfully exportable Technicolor furbelows full of Cotswold centenarians, and Chelsea Pensioners who've made the Brighton Pavilion out of matchsticks. I sat down. The lights dimmed. And on to the screen, in several shades of grey, came Waterloo Station, wrapped up by Edgar Anstey and John Schlesinger in a package called *Terminus*. Leaden-faced people milled about in the gritty air; a small boy sat on a battered trunk, and howled; queues of people moaned about trains that had left ages before, and failed to arrive. I pulled up my coatcollar. I heard the familiar dark laughter breaking out around me. And when a party of convicts appeared and shuffled into a carriage labelled: 'HOME OFFICE PARTY', I stood up slowly, mumbled; 'Excuse me' in a deep southern accent, and left. The manager was still in the lobby.

'Where're you going?' he said. 'You'll miss *Terminus*.'

'You're wrong,' I said. 'I've been there before. It's where I get off.'

He looked at me. 'You British and your sense of humour,' he said, unsmiling. 'Personally, I never went for it. But, by God, I guess you need it, huh?'

'Yes,' I said. 'I guess we do.'

Land of the Free

When, as usual, I dropped into Eat City for my morning coffee, I found Wiggins reading a letter. Or, rather, staring at it gloomily. I sat down, and he said, not looking up:

'Blighters are opening up shop in the Old Country.' The half of his doughnut which had been immersed in his coffee detached itself from the rest, and sank, with a faint plop. 'Trading stamps!' said Wiggins viciously. He shook the letter. 'My sister in Cheltenham's going to save up for a telly with them, she says. God help her!' He began to chew on the remnant of doughnut, miserably.

Having heard the news myself some weeks earlier, I'd been apprehensive about the way Wiggins would take it. Wiggins is a professional Englishman. He emigrated to Los Angeles after the war, landed a job in the P.R. department of a small film company on the strength of his accent, and, at a time when bona fide Englishmen were relatively scarce in the celluloid city, got himself elected to a place in the Hollywood cricket team by virtue of his occasional china-men. His bliss, however, lasted only a few short seasons, and was cruelly amputated by the arrival of a lighting-technician from Bolton, who, in addition to being able to turn the ball better than Wiggins, had a brother in Vancouver who shipped him a crate of bottled Bass every week. Utterly disgusted that his place in the side should have been usurped as a direct result of what was beyond question a pincer movement of Hollywood corruption and the rise of the working-classes, Wiggins drew stumps, moved to San Francisco, and found a job in a travel agency, where he now attempts to persuade Americans to visit Southern England. In his spare time, he lectures to the Daughters of the British Empire on the contamination of Albion from without, and the cataclysmic subversion of the ochlocracy within. Since, in Wiggins's view, the advent of the Green Stamp in England exemplified both, I could understand his misery.

'Cheltenham!' cried Wiggins bitterly. 'You'd have thought *they'd* have put up a bit of a show, wouldn't you? 'Fore you know where you are, they'll be flying a bloody Blue Stamps banner over Welly B.'

He sighed leadenly, gathered up his back numbers of *Country Life*, and left.

Now, although I rarely go along with Wiggins's jaundiced bleats, I was, in this case, on his side. It is early days yet in the Stamp War, and, while it required the threat of its outbreak in England to shake Wiggins, I have been worried by it, and its implications, for some time. Actual combat is a recent development; although one company, S. & H. Green Stamps, began operations in 1896, only in the past couple of years have serious competitors appeared in the field, until now their emblazonry flutters above every shopping centre, while below the flagpoles ignorant armies clash by arc-lights. And – since even Wiggins would hesitate to ascribe to Englishmen the qualities necessary to save them from the approaching Armageddon – I feel it my duty to delineate the modus operandi of the Stampmen, and the human fallibilities at which their attack is directed. The first point to note, and the essential one, is the retroaction of the American economy (which every schoolboy knows about) to a system of trust and credit; it is some time ago now that Americans lost faith in specie, and returned to marking things up on a piece of birchbark, custody of which was taken, for a small fee, by certain Elders of the Tribe, and a new hierarchy was established on the basis, not of actual wealth, but of the member's Credit Rating. Acting upon this system, the Stampmen are now working to familiarise the People with a new, more sophisticated system, the barter of actual goods. No more striking evidence of the loss of faith in money is needed than the success of the Trading Stamp, which offers a one per cent dividend on investment, and is redeemable for goods, over the Co-operative Society, which offers between two and three per cent, but returns only mere money.

Explain this discrepancy to the average American house-wife, and she will smile secretly and turn away, as women do, or, at best, say: 'If I had the money, I'd only spend it.' This is unanswerable. There is, of course, great comfort in always having one's choice directed, in knowing that one is forced to accept luxuries because one has no alternatives.

A second significant point is the special status that stamp-collections and their owners possess at a time when coin is all but valueless. For example, if one has a new TV set, it is extremely difficult to impress visitors, since the thing either cost a paltry two hundred dollars, or, more likely, came on credit. If, however, one can say: 'Oh, *that*? Why, we got that from the Green Stamps people', it means that not only did the set cost twenty thousand dollars, spent in a short period, but also that one lives, eats, and drinks, in a fashion that makes the Medicis look like coolies. There are obvious dangers, naturally; all over the States, men and women are eating themselves into early graves to buy their kiddies bicycles and dolly's tea-sets.

To go back to the question of barter and the replacement of money as the medium of exchange, I want to explain that the supermarkets carry on their phase of the War, not by cutting prices, as in the bad old days, but by creating 'Specials' on slow-selling articles, and giving stamp-bonuses for them; the profit accruing to the purchaser, of course, is less than under the Old Regime of price-reductions, since now both the Stampman, and the manufacturer of the gift-goods, must get their slices out of the cake. Also, in this lunatic development of the competitive society, it is no longer a simple question of the shopkeepers competing with one another, but also the various fraternities of Stampmen, and, beyond them, the producers of the gifts for the Stamp-men, who are carrying on the fight. Still, these logistical problems, though terrifying, are nothing to the actual battles in the field; the one I describe is typical.

The theatre of operations is a large suburban Shopping Plaza, a few acres of parking-lot enclosed on three sides by blocks of shops and supermarkets. Above these, the regimental escutcheons strain at the mast-head, bright in the sun – Thrifty Stamps, Blue Chips, Plaid Stamps, Evergreen, S. & H., and so on. In the morning air, an uncanny stillness. 09.00. The parking-lot is half-full with cars. Milling around

121

the vacant area are several hundred housewives, each in command of a shining metal trolley. The shops are open, but, as yet, empty.

09.03. From U-Shop (N.W. corner of the square, Thrifty Green) a loudspeaker opens up with a special bonus on cases of tinned ham. Immediately, a stirring flash of three hundred trolleys wheel around, swung N.W. by their commanders, and charge across the square. A dreadful rattle of armour, which drowns the screams of the slow, lame and elderly caught unprepared in the front ranks. Within seconds, U-Shop is packed full, and the rearguard is fighting hand-to-hand on the sidewalk in front.

09.10. U-Save (S.E. corner, Blue Chips) announces a bonus stamp offer on all orders over one hundred dollars. Before the tin echo has died, the erstwhile rearguard has reformed and is thundering back across the square, weaving between cars, grinding down any wounded still on the field, while from U-Shop comes the terrible sound of women being hurled into pyramids of cans. The assistant manager comes out, feet first, through a plate-glass window. A woman in a Goggomobil is rash enough to be driving into the carpark across the path of the cavalry; for five seconds, while they charge on, bits of wreckage fly up above the square, turning in the sun. When the charge is past, part of the transmission and one headlamp lie on the ground. Of the driver there is no sign.

09.13. Before U-Save is full, U-Win (N.E. corner, Evergreen) calls a special on hundred-pound vats of oleomargarine, and half the cavalry swings around in full gallop, only to meet the last of the stragglers from U-Shop (N.W.) who have managed to hack their way out and are now pounding along the sidewalk towards U-Win. However, battered as they are from the initial attack, they are no match for the relatively fresh ex-U-Savers. (Indeed, many of the U-Shoppers are now without trolleys, and are carrying cases of tinned ham on their backs) and their brave flanking action is utterly destroyed when U-Gain (between N.W. and N.E. corners) opens up a withering cross fire in Plaid Stamp bonuses on ton-sacks of old potatoes, which is the clincher for the newly-arrived legions who have been waiting outside the carpark for the Deal-Of-The-Day. Thus, in fifteen minutes the flower of suburban womanhood lies broken on the field, and the Retreat from Stalingrad is strictly a back number in the memory of Man.

Yesterday, I met in the street the woman from the apartment next to mine. She was pushing a croquet-set on a trolley, and, since she's new on crutches, I took it from her, and we walked home together.

'I've been to the Redemption Store,' she mumbled through the bandages that swathed her face. 'I got that for four books of stamps.'

'A bargain,' I said, looking at the dividend on four hundred dollars. 'Bit cramped for croquet in the flat, though, isn't it?'

'All they had for four books,' she said. 'Difficult number.'

We reached the block, and I helped her up the stairs, and opened her door for her. She looked at me out of her one good eye.

'Thank you,' she said. 'Merry Christmas!'

'Merry Christmas!' I said. I was on the point of wishing her a prosperous New Year, but something held me back. I have no idea what it was, but, now I think about it, I'm glad it did.

Through a Glass, Darkly

The man who owned the papershop came out on to the
pavement and watched me copying down addresses from
his board. He didn't say anything; he had been studying me
from inside the shop for a long time; I'd seen his eyes in the
slit between the halfdrawn blind and the Coca-Cola sign.

I took down half a dozen names and numbers and closed
my notebook. He stepped forward.

'Excuse me,' he said, a little hesitantly. He was a short,
tubby, midfortyish negro in a pinstripe blue suit, white shirt.

'Yes?' I said.

'Look buddy, maybe it ain't none of my business, but you
sure – I mean, like absolutely *sure* – you wanna look up
them addresses? What I mean is, you wanna *live* there?'

'That's right.'

'Y'ain't looking up for somebody else, maybe?'

'No. For me.'

He plucked a small cigar from his breast pocket, picked a
hair off it carefully, struck at match on his window, and lit
up, watching me through the smokeclouds.

'We – ell – ' he said, soft southern, rolling the word,
' – guess you know y'own mind. Good luck.'

'Thanks,' I said, and would have probed him, but he'd
disappeared inside the shop again, and I was left on my
blasted heath wondering whether, perhaps, he couldn't have
fitted me out with a quiet little country thaneship somewhere.

Nowhere, actually, could be less like a blasted heath than
Harlem; it is perhaps the most undeserted area in the world,
if you know what I mean. Sixlane avenues are whittled

down to alleyways by the permanent overflow from the pavements, solid, sluggish streams of people, whose reasons for being there at all seem incomprehensible – they walk too slowly to be actually *going* from A to B; they are too far from the shops and bars to have any possible interest in them; and they never appear to cross from one side of the street to the other; instead, they roll on, as if on some enormous conveyor-belt, with no apparent purpose, and no pause. Naturally, this sort of jay-walking would be treated in downtown New York as an offence located somewhere on the books between child-rape and dope-addiction; but here, a crack regiment would be needed to enforce the laws; it's left to the motorist to keep up a constant cacophanous alert to save himself from being devoured. It's an odd sensation to stand in the centre of one sidewalk looking across the slowly passing heads towards the other; the mass of humanity makes the traffic invisible, so that one seems to be cut off from the opposite bank by an open chasm filled with a perpetual honking moan, on either side of which the silent souls trudge on. Once, I thought I saw, across the gorge, Beatrice waiting in the crowd; but I must have been mistaken.

I find Harlem extremely disturbing, this sort of set-aside Negro metropolis, a sophisticated ghetto; although one rarely sees a white face, one constantly *thinks* one has, due to the fanatic attempts to approximate to the White Condition, through dress, and make-up, and hairstyling, and accent; the shops are stacked with advertised encouragement – with bleaching-creams and hairstraightening preparations and almost-white plaster models in tennis clothes. And the billboards flash products whose saleability depends upon the obvious air of success exuded by the figures depicted; and these are, without exception, the palest of negroes, often with blonde wavy hair, since these, in the hierarchy of shades which operates here, are the Top People. Constantly, the Madison Avenue stage-whisper is: This product will help you pass for White. Everything is angled towards the dispossession of the negro, towards making him a racial and cultural mongrel, towards offering him, in packet-form, an unrealisable dream. One knows that these techniques were developed to work within the tension of class-difference; but this is not the same thing at all.

I had decided to live in Harlem partly because of its proximity to Columbia University, partly because of my eviction from my Greenwich Village broomcupboard, an eviction supposed to be temporary, but as the period stated was to allow the Exterminator to rid my room of cockroaches, I decided to forego the option. (I waited to see The Exterminator. I imagined a long cadaverous Kafka-esque terror with a stovepipe hat and a little black bag and an Instrument. He turned out to be two squat toughs from Brooklyn in green overalls, who were, without question, Steiger and Brando down on their luck.)

Anyway, I was tired of the Village; as in Hampstead, or Chelsea, rents rise relative to the immigration of wealthy non-artists hunting for charm, or social cachet, or whatever it is. But here there is no Belsize Park to retire to. I was getting pushed nearer and nearer the Bowery, and since I can do without this sort of pressure to follow my natural predisposition, I determined to get out for good. Harlem is cheap.

After I left the papershop, I tried five of the addresses. I was met with the same responses at each. Surprise (one woman laughed through the gap in the door, and vanished, and wouldn't come back; but I could hear her laughing in the hall); suspicion ('Look, fellah, thanks anyway, but we got so much goddam detergent in this house, we use it to stuff pillows!'); and finally, refusal. The room, sorry, was taken. Just this minute.

The sixth address was a tall brownstone, hung with black balcony-rails and fire-escapes, an external skeleton, like a scorpion's. The door was opened by a tall, slim, grey-haired, well-dressed negro. In his lapel was a N.A.A.C.P. button. He smiled, and it was the first straight smile I'd had all morning.

'I've come about the room,' I said.

'Oh!' He looked past my shoulder into the street. 'Afraid it's taken. Guy just left.'

'Are you sure?' He looked back at me. 'Yours is the sixth place I've tried, and they were all dated this morning, and they've all gone. Odd that, isn't it?'

'Kind of.' He shifted his weight, leaning on the door-jamb. 'Big demand for rooms, though.' He looked at me, hard. 'You English?'

'That's right.'

He pushed open the door with his shoulder, and stepped back into the dark hallway.

'Look, come in for a minute, anyhow. Maybe I can help you.'

I followed him into his living-room. On one wall, a huge photograph of Martin Luther King, and a daguerrotype of John Brown. On a side-table, the latest issues of *The Southern Patriot* and *Ebony*. I sat down, and at eye-level in the bookcase were volumes of Baldwin, and Ellison, and titles like *The Negro Vanguard* and *The Truth Shall Make Us Free*. The man sat down on the arm of the chair opposite.

'Look here,' he said. 'I lied. I got a room. It's still free. Only I'm not so sure I can let you have it.'

'How come?'

He picked up one of the magazines, and fiddled with its pages.

'Look, don't get me wrong – you're a foreigner, otherwise I wouldn't have to explain. I don't want you to go thinking I'm – well, prejudiced, or anything like that.'

'You mean you don't take whites?'

'Don't say "you" like that.' He frowned, and put down the magazine. 'It's not just me. If I had my way, why, sure, I'd take you in. But I got other things to consider.'

'Such as?'

'Well, like I said, it's not me. It's the neighbours.' He looked at me, eyebrows raised in appeal. 'How're they going to feel about it? A man doesn't live alone, y'know. And this isn't just any old neighbourhood. No offence meant – but this is a pretty good-class street.'

'I know,' I said. 'That's why I like it.'

He shook his head.

'Man can't always have everything he likes. Take me – I get on fine with you people. I was in the war with white boys, fought right alongside 'em; you couldn't wish for better soldiers. I work with white people right now. They pull their weight same as the rest of us. I got white acquaintances – why, I count them among my closest friends. They come here all the time, we sit around, chew a lot of fat; you know the sort of thing.'

'Only you wouldn't have one living in your house?'

He sighed.

'I'm gonna level with you. Suppose you were to come and live here. You got white friends, right?'

I nodded.

'Okay. Pretty soon, they're gonna start visiting here regular. Maybe some of 'em'll get to like the area; why not? What then? Maybe they'll take it into their heads to move in. What the other people in the street gonna do? I'll tell you. They kinda respect me, know what I mean? I do a lot of work for them, address meetings, all that stuff. So they see I got a white boy living here. They'll reckon it's okay. So maybe they'll let your buddies move in. Pretty soon, we're gonna have us a – you'll excuse me – a white neighbourhood. I mean, let's face it, that's the way you folks are, am I right? Soon as a couple of you take hold, next thing you know there's a whole colony.'

'Well, would – I mean, is that so terrible, after all?'

He looked at me as if I were a child who'd misspelled 'cat'.

'Don't stop there, though, does it? I've lived in white areas, see? Like Greenwich Village. Now, I don't like those people who say that white men are all no-good drunks and loafers – but I've seen 'em on paynights down there, blind drunk, shouting and singing, running after women. I don't say there aren't good and bad, nor that coloured people don't behave that way sometimes. But there's no point, far as I can see, in having a lot of people like that coming in and raising hell.' He leaned forward. 'Lot of white men find coloured girls pretty attractive, huh?'

Caught either way. All right.

'Some. Like any other girls, I suppose.'

'That's just it! They're not. See what I mean? Pretty soon they're gonna start walking out together. Maybe even get married.'

'Well, even if things go that far, would that be so bad?'

He pursed his lips.

'Look, I'm liberal, like I say. I know all the reasons, too, and about love and all that, and skin not mattering, and the same blood, and so on. Except – ' he shook his head, and gave a small laugh, ' – it still kinda goes against the grain, thinking of a coloured girl going to bed with a white man. No offence?'

'No offence,' I said.

'If I had my way, I'd like to see everyone getting along

128

together, next door to one another. But – I can see you're a man of the world, an intelligent human being – you don't expect me to be the first, do you? A man has to live.'

'I suppose you're right. I don't expect you to be the first.'

'Sure you don't.' He smiled comfortably now, relieved. 'It's been interesting talking to you.' He stood up, and we went into the dim hall. 'Good to see you understand. About the room and all. But I guess that's nothing new to you; a man who's been around must've run into this sort of thing from time to time?'

'Yes,' I said, 'it all sounds pretty familiar.'

We shook hands on the step, and he closed the front door. I walked down the stone stairway, and two little coloured boys chasing one another down the street sidestepped to dodge out of my way. I took the list of addresses out of my pocket, and screwed it up, and threw it in the gutter.

Unbalance of Power

San Diego: *A woman seven-months pregnant, convicted of plotting to electrocute her husband by rigging his electric toothbrush, won probation yesterday.*

San Francisco Chronicle

My hostess leaned against a white Cadillac, and, shielding her eyes from the Hollywood sun, looked at my car.

'No *air*-conditioning?' She laughed. 'Darling, be serious!'

'I am,' I said, chastened, having arrived in Beverley Hills after a three-month cross-country trip, during which the Chevrolet had been home, mother and mistress to me. I had slept on her enormous seats, and she had seen to it, by arrangement with Drive-In restaurants, banks, stores, laundries, movies, and the like, that I was fed, clothed, entertained, and generally cosseted; I stood deeply in her debt. True, as she rested now, dwarfed by three Cadillacs, I could see that she wasn't as soignée, perhaps, as some, but for a relationship like ours, more was required than just a pretty face.

'Of course, it's a very *dependable* little car.' This sop thrown to my chagrin sounded too much like: 'Oh, I'm sure she'll make him a good wife and housekeeper, and all that, but . . . ' to console me. A servant, pushing my tattered luggage on a gleaming trolley, disappeared into the great glass palace, and the young woman took my arm.

'I'm sorry there's no one to welcome you properly,' she said, 'the family's taking its siesta.' A glass door flew open as we approached, and shut behind us. Inside, the house was cool, and silent, except for a muted humming. 'I'm sure you're utterly exhausted by the heat – nobody'll be up for hours, so why don't I show you to your room and let you recover?'

I trailed her down a glass-roofed tube, our steps noiseless in thick pile. She stopped; a portion of wall slid open at her touch.

'It isn't *très luxe*,' she said coyly, 'but at least it's *gemütlich*.'

It was about as *gemütlich* as the Alhambra, but I am too poised a cosmopolite to gasp openly.

'That's your dressing-room,' she said. 'And there's the bathroom. Ring if you need anything. All the buttons are on the headrest. If the air's too cool, the top dial adjusts it. The relaxer works from the small blue box on the left of the phone.'

'The what?'

She pointed it out to me. After she had left, and I had managed to find my way into the immense circular bed, I stared at the box for some time. It bore the legend: 'Sleep-E-Zee' and swore it would gentle me into the Soundest Slumber. Since my childhood was filled with cautionary tales about little boys who'd switched on the light while standing in the bath, or gone climbing things, only to be fused into a permanent part of the National Grid, I have grown up with a healthy suspicion of creeping electricity; I used an electric blanket once, and spent the whole night lying awake, waiting for the 'Ping!' that would shoot me out of the end of the bed, delicately browned on both sides. But the 'Sleep-E-Zee' tempted; I have, for one thing, never been gentled. I pressed the switch. Immediately, the bed began to undulate, and I with it. But not for long. I felt like Ahab, lashed to Moby Dick on the long last ride, and distinctly Un-E-Zee. I dismounted, and stood by while the great silken disc shimmied and hummed, until, having made certain that it had finished gentling for the day, I crawled back in, and finally slept.

I awoke to a bell chiming near my head. When I'd worked out why, I lifted the blue receiver.

'Hi! I'm Bob – sorry I wasn't up to welcome you. Sleep O.K.?'

'Fine,' I said.

'Thought you might like to catch the ball-game. Dodgers are in, bases loaded, bottom of the fifth. It's the button under the phone. See you before dinner.' He rang off.

I pushed the button, out of curiosity, and the screen embedded in the facing wall flickered; men were chasing one another around a green diamond, while a hysterical scream explained things inexplicably. I switched off. The phone rang again.

'See *that*! In a mile on third, and he's called!'

Bob rang off. I relaxed a moment, then let the receiver dangle from its cord, and padded into the bathroom.

While I was lathering my face, there was a knock at the door.

'Come in!'

'I cun't getch'onna phone,' said a small boy's voice. 'Mom said to bring y'a toothbrush.' He appeared in the doorway, and I felt his stare. I looked down, smiling. For a second, he stood paralysed; then he turned and fled; I heard him screaming in the corridor.

'HE'S CUTTING HIS FACE OFF! MOM, HE'S CUTTING HIS FACE OFF WITH A KNIFE!'

A moment later, his mother's voice asked if I were decent.

'Pyjamas,' I replied, whereupon the room filled with children, all dressed in nightclothes. Apparently, in this house where everything gravitated towards the bed, pyjamas were de rigueur. The five children, aged between four and eleven, assembled, staring behind their mother. She laughed.

'It's all right, darlings,' she giggled, 'he's only shaving.'

The littlest boy, who'd discovered the butchery, complained.

'But he isn't plugged in.'

'Once upon a time, everybody shaved like that, Winslow.'

It was as if I'd been caught putting the finishing touches to my woad. The mother handed me a box, smiled, and left. The children lingered. Inside the box was a plastic cylinder the size of a torch, with a bristled head. I looked enquiringly at the audience. The eldest girl took it from me, unwound its cord, and plugged it into the wall. Instantly, the bristles agitated frantically.

'It's the guest-brush,' said the girl. 'With your personal head.'

'Thanks, but I have my own toothbrush,' I said, producing it. The room rocked with hysterical convulsions; the two youngest children rolled on the floor, choking. The eldest girl controlled herself.

'You can't use *that*!' she insisted. 'No one uses those any more. They're unhygienic. They give you cavities. They don't massage. And they're hard *work*. They're not *electric*,' she finished, decisively. Then she added as an afterthought: 'The Squibb Automatic does in three minutes what used to take five.'

'What do you do with the other two minutes?' I asked, but she'd turned away in disgust. The other children had lost interest in their Neanderthaler; three of them were on my bed, one of them switching the TV on and off, one pummelling her tummy with an electric masseur, one sending the venetian blinds shooting up and down. The eight-year-old boy was apparently phoning his date. The scene resembled those displays at the Kensington Science Museum where one touches a button and a miniature power-station is galvanised into sudden crazed activity.

Now, I'm not against luxury and labour-saving as such; God knows, it's about the only thing Progress has given us, and we ought to cherish it, especially since we may one day be called upon to pay in full for the scientific upthrust of which the Automatic Toothbrush is merely a delightful by-product. Nor do I object to attention lavished on beds. But total dependence on these things is an altogether different story. As I stood there, trusting in my ancient Wisdom to brush my teeth, I wondered what the effects of a prolonged power-cut would be on this household. Presumably, they would be incarcerated in their glittering pile, behind the now unopenable doors, each in his or her motionless bed, unable to Slumber Soundly, lying there with their teeth mouldering, the paterfamilias hideously bearded, everyone sweltering in the heat, incapable of opening the electric windows, while the food supplies rotted in the freezer, uncookable on the heatless stove. I suppose – and I assume that the phone-lines would be similarly defunct – that eventually they would struggle from their beds, and beat feebly against the plate-glass walls, until hunger or airlessness finally and mercifully overcame them.

But it required far less than this extremity to drive the lady in my head-quotation over the brink. The primary *N.E.D.*

definition of 'Electricity' is: 'The state of excitation produced by friction.' This, then, is her disease. She suffered from Electricity; and its final stages were probably these:

It is Sunday morning in San Diego, in the house of – let's call them Mr. and Mrs. Oblomov. Mrs. D. has spent a wretched night; she is a light sleeper, whereas her husband insists on keeping the Sleep-E-Zee bucking all night; she likes to leave the windows open, for warm air, but he must have the room hermetically sealed and icy; in consequence, she has been sitting in an armchair since 1 a.m. Dawn breaks, and she crawls exhaustedly into bed. As she drops off, Oblomov wakes, turns off the machine (to which she has just acclimatised herself) and switched on the TV. She pulls a pillow over her head. He begins to shave with one hand, massaging his scalp with the other, setting up a two-pitch buzz. Beaten, she drags herself into the kitchen to prepare breakfast; all around her, toast leaps from toasters, electric kettles boil over, alarms ring; every two minutes, Oblomov phones, demanding food. She drops into a chair, which begins to rock her electrically, her face buried in her hands. Every day, it is the same. She can stand it no longer. And then an idea forms in her diseased mind, subtly. She lifts her head slowly, smiling diabolically. The fitness of it appeals to her. There is poetry left in the soul of Mrs. Oblomov. She takes her husband's electric toothbrush from the shelf, and goes to work on it with a nail-file. Satisfied, she fills a bowl with water, and carried brush and bowl into the bedroom.

'Darling,' she says sweetly, 'as a special treat, I thought you'd like to brush your teeth without getting up this morning.'

Well, she bungled the job, and got probation. And I'm glad. Not that I think Oblomov deserves anything but instant liquidation. But if she'd succeeded in her noble designs, only to have society strap her into the Electric Chair, I think it would have broken my heart.

The Dog in the
Grey Flannel Suit

Hardening of the arteries, heart attacks, and other human ailments are spreading to the poodle population of America, because of the pampering many of them receive.

The Times

Well, doc, you know, up and down, up and down. I cured the tic, though. Yeah, I beat it, ha-ha. Okay, we beat it. You'll never know how grateful . . . sure I have to say it. I mean, it was like I was turning into some kind of a nut, or something. That's how it looked to people. Well, you know how people are, doc, I mean I don't have to draw you a . . . I mean, with my whole lousy face twitching and my hat falling off all the goddam time. The homburg. Yeah, that's the one. With the grey felt . . . oh, really? Like Joseph Cotton? Ha-ha, I think you're maybe having a little fun at my expense . . . please don't get offended, I know you guys have high overheads, I didn't mean . . . I mean, I don't give a damn about the money. Just so's I get to, you know, talk to you once in a while. That's it, doc. Communicate.

It's damn funny about that tic and my mother, wouldn't you say? I mean, how many fellas my age got a mother, she had this tic in her face, my old man used to knock hell out of her for? Like, who'd ever believe it? Doc, I didn't say that, did I? *I* believe it . . . I have to hand it to you headshrinkers, you certainly know . . . it's a figure of speech, doc, that's all. Sort of a figure of speech, see? Sure I like you.

135

How much? *That* much! Okay, just a teensy-weensy bit more, ha-ha-ha. How's that?

The dog? No, I guess I won't leave him outside. It's just off his paws, doc. It's been raining, see? I swear that's all it is. It's about Burton I came to see you. Yeah, *Burton*. Burton, say hello to the nice psychiatrist. No, I guess he isn't too talkative at that. He has this problem. No, the halitosis we can cure. Burton has this emotional problem . . . look, doc, we're *all* busy men. For twenty-five bucks a throw, does it matter whose problems we talk about?

Well, like I was saying last time about the tic and Momma beating me and everything . . . Momma, doc. My wife. Look, doc, it's all there on my goddam card. Lemme see that . . . that's my brother's card you got there doc. Willie. The klepto. I'm Joe. The one with the tic. That's it, the grey homburg. Okay, so like I said, Momma and me stopped, you know, doing things after that time I got passed over for the directorship, and she started on about my loss of power, and how could she resp . . . doc, you're telling *me* she has a funny way of looking at power? My wife has a funny way of *breathing*, for Christ's sake.

So it got so's our way of life was, well, re-arranged a little. Momma took to eating, and I began to stay . . . no, just eating. Anything. Hell, she has a treble chin you could hang your hat on. And going to seances, psychiatrists, that sort of thing. I *know* there's a difference, doc, I'm just giving you a for-instance, okay? Right. Me, I took to staying late at the office. Yeah, we make those Rock-U automatic mattresses with the adjustable rhythm . . . please, doc, this ain't my day for funny stories. Anyway, I had a nice little thing going for me, with this kid, you know, this girl from the typing-pool . . . look, my friend, everybody adjusts in his own way, right? I mean, how much emotional capital's a guy supposed to sink into a wife against a twice-a-year dividend on investment. Not when there's a Blue Chip issue right there in front of you, ha-ha-ha.

Sure I tried hard with Momma. I don't need no sermons, doc, those I pick up gratis on Sundays. First City Church of Christ the Industrialist, and you? Oh. Well, you don't look it, if it's any comfort. I tried with Momma, see? I don't have any guilt-feelings on that score. I got us this apartment in the East Seventies, genuine Persian wall-to-wall, colour TV in every bathroom, Multivox stereo. By God, doc, d'you realise Momma had music day and night at the touch of a lousy button?

Oh, yeah, she changed. I mean, we didn't have no more fights, and it got so she used to be waiting for me when I got back at midnight, with a martini all fixed, and wearing this gold-lamé get-up, like . . . like some kid from a typing-pool, or something. I wish you coulda seen her, doc, I mean this old doll done up like a Christmas tree. I mean, I had to laugh, didn't I? Boy, came her fortieth birthday, did *she* get scared! Funny thing, there was times, I almost felt sorry for her.

So she went off on this loneliness kick, see? That was about the time I had to make the Tokyo trip. I bought her this budgerigar, it could recite the Gettysburg address and sing the baritone part on *Sweet Adeline*. I get back from Tokyo after a month, and what do I find? I find two hundred bucksworth of natural talent, flat on its little back with its feet in the air. And Momma, just staring out of the window. So I take the bird down to a vet, and he say's its dead, but for 3.95 he'll do an autopsy in case I should want to sue the shop . . . he said it was the first budgerigar he'd ever seen dead from cirrhosis. It had enough stuffed olives in its little gut to feed a carthorse.

After that I got her this cat. It was more of a *thing*, know what I mean? Not that it could sing, mind you, but it so happens that Momma sings baritone herself, so she didn't get much joy out of the budgie, anyway. Everything was fine for a while. I'd get home weekends, and I'd find Momma and the cat curled up in front of the late-late show. Only pretty soon, they'd begin to start talking, see? I mean, I'd be in bed and I'd hear Momma chewing the ear of this god-dam moggy, all about her miscarriages, and how she'd like to go round the world, see Tokyo, that sort of thing. About how crummy it was getting old, and all sorts of crap she'd picked up from *Reader's Digest*. At first, I got sick of listening to it, night after night, but then I figured, what the hell, as long as she's happy? Anyway, the cat develops this ulcer, see? So we had it put down, swell funeral, black clothes, the lot. Boy, I'm telling you, doc, if cats have a heaven, that rotten tabby is Mister Status himself.

Which brings us to Burton. That's right, doc, the dog. I

bought him for her six months ago, and what with me not stopping by more than once a month or so, she and him have gotten pretty close. Only this time, when I get home, I find this poor little animal sitting on this Louis Kwinz chair we have, wearing a little pinstripe suit and a grey homburg hat, smoking a Meerschaum. Me, I'm no expert on poodles, but he don't look good to me. I mean, he don't bark, he don't sniff, now he don't even eat. Every time she comes into the room, he throws up. Most of the time, he just stares at the carpet while she screams at him.

I tell you, doc, you have to help him. If anything happened to the dog, I'd never forgive myself.

The Man Who Ran
for President

The heap of flyblown rags sitting opposite me in the Bowery flophouse pushed a battered tin across the booze-sodden table.

'Cigarette?' he said. His shrivelled claw plucked at the lid, and I peered down into a goulash of yellow dog-ends and frayed cigar-butts. 'Go on, I dried 'em myself.'

We lit up, and forcing down the emetic tang of old bus-stations and Skid Row gutters that clogged my throat, I called the barman over and ordered a jar of the best wood-alcohol in the house. He shuffled away across the festering mounds of supine clientèle, and I turned again to the Man Who Ran For President.

'It's a great honour to meet you, sir,' I said.

He plucked a fishbone from his clotted beard and examined it thoughtfully.

'Thank you, son,' he replied. A frisson ran through me at the memories called up by those rolling Texan cadences. I knew greatness when I saw it. 'Don't mind mah calling you son?' He waved his hand around the stew. 'They are all my sons.'

I choked back a timely sob. An ancient mouldering bum stumbled past, and my companion caught him by the edge of his groundsheet.

'How yuh doing, Charlie?' he cried.

The old wino's face lit up briefly, like something hanging on a ghost train wall.

'You coulda bin the greatest goddam President we ever had,' he said. 'You coulda bin on 4c. stamps and everything.'

He limped on, belching, into the fetid gloom.

'See?' said the Man Who Ran For President. 'He remembers. They all remember.' He blew his nose sadly, pinching it between thumb and forefinger with that characteristic mixture of panache and grace that I recalled so well from the old newsreels. A lump formed beneath my tonsils. He had come so close to greatness, once.

'Tell me,' I said, pouring a generous measure of rotgut into his saucer, 'what drives men to run for the Presidency?'

He peered at me, his blue pupils twinkling in their plummy aspic, and smiled.

'I'll tell you an old story, son,' he murmured, his voice like moonlight, fine, along the Wabash. 'When Andy Jackson was runnin' for President in 1828, his campaign tour took him through Illinois. At every meeting he addressed, there in the front row, a lean-faced, ganglin' boy was always sittin', staring up at Andy with awe and reverence in his young eyes. Now, at the end of his last meeting, Jackson stepped down from the dais and walked over to where the boy was sitting.

' "Tell me, son," he said, 'how come a sprat like you sits in on every damn one of my meetings?"

' "Because,' said the boy, "one day I'm gonna be up there on the platform, and I'm gonna be President, and I'm gonna make this great country one nation under God."

' "I see,' said Jackson. "And what's your name, son?"

' "Abe," said the boy.

' "Abe what?"

'The youth squared his skinny shoulders.

' "Abe Grodzinsky, sir," he said.'

The Man Who Ran For President shook his head, and I shook mine, and we stared for a while at a spot in the centre of the table, thinking many things.

'Had it all in the palm of mah hand,' he said at last. 'Man gits so close he kin spit on the White House, and what happens?'

'What?' I said.

The M.W.R.F.P. drew a crude map of North America in spilt booze, and sighed.

'You remember when I got the Presidential nomination at the party convention?'

I nodded.

'It was a landslide. The Party hadn't ever seen anybody like me. I was the American Dream, see? I was Horatio Alger and Charlie Lindbergh and Li'l Abner and Shirley Temple and George Washington, all rolled into one. I mean, my grandfather was the only coloured rabbi ever to win an Olympic gold medal, my uncle made it to cardinal before he was thirty, my sister was Playmate of the Year and a double-agent for the F.B.I., my brother was the first boss of the Teamsters' Union ever to get a religious record in the hit parade, and my Irish father won the Medal of Honour before opening a chain of cut-price liquor stores across the country. Apart from giving all its money to charity, my family had a tradition of political and moral leadership that made the Adams's and the Kennedys look like the Beverly Hillbillies.'

The Man Who Ran For President broke off suddenly in a rattle of old lungs, and, bravely, I smiled through my tears while he recovered.

'And *me*?' he went on ' – I had six-three, a hunnerd and eighty pounds, All-American Footballer, Pulitzer Poetry-Prizewinner, a Fellow of Harvard – and, believe me, son, no other cordon bleu cook is gonna swim the English Channel both ways in *our* lifetime.'

He slipped a benzedrine tablet under his tongue gloomily, and chased it down with a shot of meths.

'In the first month of my campaign, I covered three thousand miles on horseback, spreading love and integrity. The press went mad. Men in Death Row broke down and cried like babies when I spoke on the radio. By the second month, I'd ironed out the whole racial problem at a campaign dinner for the K.K.K. and the N.A.A.C.P. Malcolm X was the guest of honour, and General Walker handed round the funny hats. Then a woman in Boise, Idaho, swore she saw stigmata on my hands during a speech on fiscal policy, and two days later the Catholic vote was home and dry. I was all things to all men, see? No one could object to me, 'cos in my soul, in the very fibres of my being, son, there was – well – a little bit of them.'

I caught a drooping lip between incisors, and hushed its trembling.

'I made speeches in Italian, Spanish, Rumanian – I held a mixed audience spellbound on the Boston waterfront, once, just by speaking German with an Irish-Kentucky drawl, and pulled in the floating Japanese vote with a coupla Haiku quotes that left 'em sobbing into their toolboxes. The second month, the Opposition nominee backed down from the race. The country was ready to lynch anyone who stood against me; anyway, most of the Opposition party members had turned in their campaign buttons to vote for me themselves.'

He paused to lick a pool from the tabletop.

'Trouble is with a democracy, son,' he continued sadly, ' – is it's made up of people.'

'True,' I said, 'true.' For it was.

'I was into the straight and runnin' for home by a walkover, when some fink stands up in public and says he knows for a fact my brother-in-law's niece kicked a dog for a bet. We had the guy committed, but it was too late. The blue-rinse vote went down the drain, and when they found out the dog was black, the Northern liberals and the coons went with 'em. I coulda maybe held the balance even then by running on a straight racist ticket and holding the South, but two days later some stinking *agent provocateur* framed my chauffeur's grandfather in the lavatory of the Washington Y.M.C.A. The only Southerners I managed to hold after that were a couple of hairdressers from Atlanta, and a playwright whose name escapes me. Even then, I coulda held the Midwest and the Pacific Coast, and made a fight of it, but the next day news broke that my third cousin had accepted the gift of a clockwork train for his eighth birthday from the friend of a man whose wife had relatives in East Berlin, and I was asked to stand down from the nomination.'

He fell suddenly silent. I finished my meths, and stood up to leave. I was going blind. I'm a pretty hard drinker, but even I know when to draw the line. I patted the Man Who Ran For President on his threadbare shoulder.

'It was an honour, sir,' I said.

He glanced up at me, moistly.

'Tell me just one thing, son,' he said softly. 'Would *you* buy a used car from a man like me?'

I nodded, stifling a sob.

142

'Sure I would. I think – I think you would have made the greatest used car dealer we ever had.'

He smiled a hero's smile.

'Thank yuh, son,' he said.

 **ME**

Behind the Curtain

We came out of Vienna late, driving East under an evening sky thick with blotchy augury. Great pulpy clouds hung low in the windlessness, like rotten plums in some gargantuan compote, sour, evil, ominous.

'Gorgeous evening,' said my wife. 'Glorious sunset.'

I smiled sardonically, locking the Truth inside me, the way a man has to, sometimes. I said, in a voice taut with what I can only describe as emotion:

'We'll be at the border in twenty minutes.'

Good word, border. I like saying words like that. In fact, now I think about it, I could even have said 'frontier'. *There's* a word for you. Not often you get the opportunity to pull a word like frontier out of the bag. Can't use it at all those chi-chi comic-operetta toy-shops you get at run-of-the-mill tourist borders in France and Switzerland, where jolly fat customsmen ogle your wife's legs and refuse to stamp your passport and speak impeccable English, and generally devalue the Romance of International travel. But here, roaring through the gathering night towards Czechoslovakia, into the unknown totalitarian forests, glancing in one's mirror at the lost horizon beyond which honest men are tucking in to teatime honey under the church-clocks, here, if anywhere, is there a justification for 'frontier'.

'Good,' said my wife. She wrenched the driving-mirror out of my reverie, and reached for her eye-shadow.

'I wouldn't advise it,' I said.

'What wouldn't you advise?'

'Make-up. Putting on make-up. We look decadent enough as it is.'

I looked away quickly, being in no mood to be despised, and returned to reflection as the last kilometres ran under the car. Wrong way to penetrate the Iron Curtain, in a shiny Western affluence-advert. Ought to cross frontiers in a mud-caked, dented Land-Rover, a travel-scarred paramilitary vehicle with spades and picks and jerrycans of brackish water strapped to the bonnet. With 'LONDON-MARRAKESH-KARACHI-VLADIVOSTOCK painted on the sides. Should be wearing sweat-stained khaki bush-shirts and shorts, set off, for preference, with a bit of clotted blood here and there, and a webbing-belt hung with compass-cases and machetes. Or else, ought to be crossing on a munitions-train, lying flat on a boxcar roof, clutching a stolen meat-axe and swearing to take half a dozen of the bastards with me if I'm caught. Not quite the same in immaculate dripdry trousers and lime-green Hush Puppies.

'How do I look?' she said.

'Terrible. Rich. Tory. Idle.'

'Thank you.'

'You look like the pointless end-product for which ten thousand starving coolies sweated in suffocating holes. And look at all that damned luggage.'

We only had two cases on the back seat, and they were just this side of derelict, at that. But in East European twilight, old plastic can look sickeningly opulent. They were cases that might have been stuffed with grey toppers and astrakhan coats and gold toothpicks and *Wall Street Journals*.

'Stop worrying,' said my wife. 'It'll be all right when they open them. Your underwear is curiously apolitical to look at.'

'Don't be too sure. There's that blasted Marks and Spencer's stuff for a start. You can see their little minds going like the clappers as soon as they see pants with "St. Michael" stamped all over them. Wouldn't surprise me if you can get ten years for wearing religious underwear.'

'You could always plead it was a deliberate act of desecration,' said my wife. 'You might end up with the Order of Lenin.'

'I wish I could impress on you the seriousness of all this.'

146

'Don't worry,' said my wife, 'you're doing fine.'

We passed the Austrian customs, and drove into No-Man's Land.

'Do you think it was absolutely necessary to shake that Austrian's hand?'

'I thought it was the sort of thing called for in the circumstances,' I said. 'He probably expected it.'

'True. I gathered as much from the way you had to shake mine to show him what you wanted him to do.'

As we approached the Czech frontier-control, I turned to her, unhurriedly, subtly, and hissed, through the bright, friendly smile I had rehearsed for the past three days in Austrian shaving-mirrors:

'They're watching us from that machine-gun post. *Don't look at them, for Christ's sake!* Pretend you haven't noticed.'

'If you mean that water-tower,' said my wife, 'they look to me as though they're painting it.'

I laughed bitterly, almost without noise.

'You happen to forget,' I whispered with motionless lips, 'that they're past masters in techniques of deception.'

'If they ever run short of ideas,' she said, 'I know where they can pick up a tip or two.'

I switched off the engine as a squat man in olive fatigues loomed up menacingly out of the dusk.

'Here they come. Take your sunglasses off. Try to remember we've got nothing to hide.'

The official saluted.

'Bonjour,' I said, slapping my thigh merrily.

He took the passports away.

' "Bonjour"?' asked my wife.

'You don't want that man to think I'm a fool, do you? If he cottons on that I'm multi-lingual, he'll think twice before pulling anything. He probably thinks I speak fluent Czech.'

She lit a cigarette.

'Try saying "muchas gracias" when he comes back,' she said. 'If that doesn't convince him, nothing will.'

The man reappeared, and, with a bow, handed her the passports.

'Can we drive off now?' she said. 'I mean, would you say it's safe to turn our backs on them? Or should we drive to Prague in reverse, throwing confetti and singing the *Internationale*? After all, you're the man with the inside dope.

147

Without you, I'd probably be refusing the blindfold right now.'

I ignored this outburst. The sudden release from pent-up fear makes people behave oddly. With an ironically raised eyebrow, a jutted chin, and the smallest of smiles playing about my lips (no small feat), I headed the car towards the lights of Bratislava, across the Danube.

'It's nine p.m.,' she said. 'If I put the radio on, we could catch the A.F.N. news from Munich.'

I beat her to the switch just in time.

'Are you out of your mind? Take a look around. The road is thick with them.'

'Who's them?'

'How the hell should I know? Red Army officers, M.V.D., double-agents – they could be anything.'

'I suppose you're right. Especially that old man with the scythe over his shoulder. And that female octogenarian with the bundle of washing. Not to mention that bunch of kids trying to look as though they're waiting for a bus. I wish we had false moustaches.'

A hare, impaled on a headlight beam, stopped dead for a second, staring blindly, before it shot away into the night.

'See that?' I said.

'Yes. He gave us a damned funny look. I wonder where they find counterspies eighteen inches tall?'

I didn't break the uneasy silence until we pulled up in front of the Hotel Devin. A gaggle of uniformed midgets broke ranks and clustered around the boot, but I shooed them away.

'I wonder if you'd mind carrying in the luggage?' I said.

'Me?'

'Create a marvellous impression. It'd look, you know, progressive. Emancipated. Help to integrate us.'

Our way through the foyer was barred by serried ranks of decolletée females, shimmying about in the perfumed air, tinkling with cocktail laughter. My wife threw down her load.

'I wish I had my old dungarees and gumboots,' she said. 'I hate to make these kids feel dowdy.'

'They're obviously the fully-paid-up mistresses of local gauleiters,' I whispered behind a deftly cupped hand.

'My heart bleeds. Just think – but for the caprice of Fate,

they could be lugging packing crates around in a democratic ecstasy like the rest of us lucky girls. I bet it's even subversive to have a heart of gold, too. What's a nice girl like me doing in a place like this?'

She smiled at the hovering porters, and they pounced on the bags. She led them to a lift, and a muted groan turned inside me. I made for the stairs, hoping enough natives would notice the attempt at image-redemption, and, by sprinting, I got to the room first. I'd managed to removed all the paintings from the walls, and was unscrewing the telephone base-plate when my wife and her entourage of capitalist lackeys pulled in. They stared at me silently for some time.

'He's looking for microphones,' she explained.

The lackeys rolled about on the carpet in uncontrollable hysteria.

'Thank you,' I said, with that dignity which passes understanding. 'Maybe if you ask them nicely at dawn tomorrow, they'll let you administer the *coup de grace*.'

The porters had composed themselves, and were leaning on things.

'And now,' I said scathingly, 'how do we get rid of the spies?'

'We tip them.'

'Bribe state officials?'

She sighed as she opened my wallet. The men began bowing, and, as she slipped an International Incident into one eager palm, the agent said: 'Right away, madame.'

'Right away what?' I asked weakly, as the door closed.

'Right away food. A little room service. Word has it that people eat in this country.'

I groped for an anchorage in the reeling room.

'Word also has it,' I gritted, 'that they nailed Lavrenti Beria for ordering a shandy after hours. In a mere sockful of minutes, you have managed to insinuate graft, corruption, greed, servitude, class and *übermenschlichkeit* into a society dedicated to their extinction.'

There was a knock at the door, and I put a match to my address book. My wife admitted a trolley and a waiter in close order, and uncovered a cold chicken, plates of assorted meats, and a well-stocked ice-bucket.

'That's the clincher,' I murmured. 'There's only one brand

of citizen who gets a meal like that behind the Curtain.'

She popped a cork.

'See you on the scaffold,' she said.

Don't think it was fear that kept me from eating. A man like me learns to face death early in his career. It's just that it takes more than a mess of pottage to make me compromise with my beliefs.

Black and White and Red All Over

A few weeks ago, I would have counted myself one with the millions of Englishmen whose credo for the future of benighted mankind is that if only the airmail edition of the *Telegraph* can get through, everything will be all right. The surest foundation, they feel, for mutual understanding between, say, Mongolia and the West, is that the chaps in Ulan Bator be given the opportunity to discover the Whole Truth, served up to them with the loving objectivity of Fleet Street. To the majority of English believers, the concept of a free press is that foreigners can get English papers; it doesn't have anything to do with what they're allowed to print on their own corrupt, illiterate native presses. And to the Briton abroad, the measure of a country's civilisation is the number of English papers available, the currency of the edition, and the size of the smallest village in which they're obtainable. I have seen them, mooning through the alien streets at what ought to be tea-time, searching for a toasted scone and clutching a tattered copy of a week-old *Daily Mirror*, whose rupture advertisements they have read ten times in a mood compounded of frustration, xenophobia and bitter nostalgia. To the more enlightened Briton, however, the unavailability of English print is more than a question of personal deprivation; what bothers him is the absence of any corrective to the filthy mythology grafted on to the British by foreign journalists. Where, they cry, is the antidote to that caricature of John Bull, the chinless cretin in the mouldering pith-helmet, the impotent anachronism that wanders the world

151

dreaming of gunboats and tea and thatch and hotwater-bottles and Windsor Castle? And nowhere, naturally, do they feel themselves to be so misrepresented as they are behind the Iron Curtain, crucified by a captive press which never sees the other fellow's point of view.

Well, as I said before, a month ago I would have gone to the wall in defence of the itinerant chauvinist and the press he worships, but that was before I'd taken my own peep behind the arras. Back now from a singularly nasty incident in Czechoslovakia, I'm inclined to think that the British image would stand up better to the Soviet bloc if we exported lamé tuxedos and plastic models of the Duke of Gloucester, rather than newspapers.

The only English paper officially available in Prague is the *Daily Worker*. To suddenly come upon it, clamped to a rack alongside *Pravda, l'Humanité*, and the wealth, if that's the right word, of thick, funfilled papers put out by other Communist parties, evokes a curious response in the English non-Communist. It's such a weedy little thing, whose main preoccupation seems always to be a heart-rending appeal for funds to keep emaciated body and soul together, that I heard more than one English tourist shooting off his mouth in the hotel paper-shop about what a disgrace it was that British Reds couldn't put up a bit better show, and how they were letting the old side down. There was, however, at least one more English paper unofficially available in Czechoslovakia on July 22, and I had it. It was a *Sunday Express*, dated July 19, picked up in Vienna for a mere exorbitance on the day I crossed the border so that I could keep abreast of developments at Walthamstow dog-track. But what with one thing and another, the first opportunity I found to look at it was on my first night in Prague, while I was tucking into a slivovicz highball in the hotel snuggery. I hadn't got much further than the moving news that the moon had risen over the *Express* at 4.52 a.m., when a voice slid into my left ear.

'Excuse me,' it said, with what I instantly identified as a high Moravian twang, 'but I wondered if I might look at your newspaper.'

I turned round very cautiously, with what, to a casual observer, might have seemed the air of a man expecting to see trenchcoats and gunbarrels, but the chap was actually a pleasant-faced young Czech in a blue suit and a wide smile.

'Of course!' I cried, leaping at this chance to shed a little phosphorescent gospel among the world's dark crannies. I laid the paper between us, and we craned sociably.

'Who is this Lord Beaverbrook who founded?' he asked.

I explained, carefully.

'So. And it is selling four million copies! Marvellous! And what is the Socialist paper that sells four million also?'

'I'm afraid I don't quite follow you.'

'For the impartiality? For the two sides of the picture? The truth.'

I racked an unfruitful brain, while he studied the front page.

'I am intrigued by this headline,' he murmured, ' "The Great John Bloom Mystery Still Grows".' He laughed. 'It is sounding like the worst excesses of capitalist duplicity, but I know from our own papers that things are no longer like this in Britain. Is this really "the dramatic fall of an empire"?'

'Well,' I said, 'not quite. But it's news, you see. Bloom is rather insignificant, but the *story* is big, if you follow me.'

'I am not sure. It is bigger than this paragraph in tiny print that the U.S. and Britain have tested another H-bomb?'

'It's just as true!' I snapped, grabbing the paper. 'Anyway, look at these big photographs, feel this luxurious paper, see these hilarious cartoons, look at all this fabulous sports-news. By heavens, we know how to live in England!'

But he was peering at the letters page, shaking his head.

'There is here what is looking like an advertisement, but this cannot be. See – "Conservatives Give You A Better Standard Of Living. Keep it!" It is just a confusion of the name, no? *Conservatives* is perhaps a brand of boiled sweets?'

'Well, as a matter of –'

'Ah. But how is it that there is an advertisement for one party and not for others? Is this freedom of press?'

'It's got nothing to do with freedom,' I said heatedly, 'it's simply that the Conservatives have got more – have got more –'

'Yes?'

'More – more *initiative* than the Socialists.'

153

He looked at me, with a strange, Czech look, and turned a page.

'Who is this Sir Gilbert Davies, this Lloyd's underwriting person who is queuing up every week for National Assistance? It says he is a company director but he is technically unemployed, and is therefore entitled to £5 9s. a week. This is obviously what is called a newspaper stunt, no? It is a joke, of course?'

'Of course,' I muttered. I snatched a large vodka, and hurled it down. It helped me to laugh.

'I am looking at this Robert Glenton questionnaire on greed,' said the young man. 'I am intrigued that the editor of the most-selling Sunday newspaper is believing that his readers are fascinated with their own greed and other people's. Can it be that wealth is not eliminating envy after all?'

'I wouldn't know,' I said. And I knew I had him cornered. 'But surely greed is just another name for ambition, isn't it?'

The clear eyes looked at me, coolly.

'Who's arguing?' he said. He looked down again at the page.

'Strange – there is an extract from Mr. Goldwater's book and he is writing: "We would rather follow the world to Kingdom Come than consign it to Hell under Communism". I cannot find editorial comment on this. Only a paragraph on the leading page which says that Goldwater is the reason why Britain should have an independent H-bomb. I am not following this line of argument.'

'It's terribly complicated,' I said quickly. 'Wouldn't you rather look at the sports-pages with all their dramatic action-packed photographs and everything?'

'No,' he said. 'I am looking rather at these pages with readers' letters and Ephraim Hardcastle, and I am discovering that the Queen's cousin has bought an island for £60,000 and that some doubt is now cast on the fact that Mr. George Strauss is England's richest Socialist, and that Belton House has been saved from dry rot at a cost of £80,000. And I am also learning that a Mr. J. T. Robson of West Didsbury is remarkably struck by the resemblance between Sir Alec Douglas-Home's wife and his grandmother. What do I want with sport-pages?'

154

'I don't know,' I said, taking the paper from him and tearing it neatly into several hundred unreadable pieces, 'I just thought you might like to get a balanced view of things, that's all.'

Under the Influence
of Literature

My mother was the first person to learn that I had begun to take literature seriously. The intimation came in the form of a note slid under my bedroom door on the morning of February 4 (I think), 1952. It said, quite simply:

Dear Mother,
Please do not be alarmed, but I have turned into a big black bug. In spite of this I am still your son so do not treat me any different. It must have happened in the night. On no account throw any apples in case they stick in my back which could kill me.

Your son.

I hasten to add that this turned out to be a lousy diagnosis on my part. But the night before I had gone to bed hugging my giant panda and a collected Kafka found under a piano leg, and since, when I woke up, I was flat on my back, it seemed only reasonable to suppose that I'd metamorphosed along with Gregor Samsa, and was now a fully paid-up cockroach. The fit passed by lunchtime, but for years my father used the story to stagger people who asked him why he was so young and so grey.

Thing is, I was pushing fourteen at the time, and caught in that miserable No-Man's-Land between Meccano and Sex, wide open to suggestions that life was hell. My long trousers were a travesty of manhood, and shaving was a matter of tweezers and hope. Suddenly aware of how tall girls were, and of how poorly a box of dead butterflies and a luminous compass fit a man for a smooth initiation into the perfumed garden, I tried a desperate crash-programme of self-taught sophistication; I spent my evenings dancing alone in a darkened garage, drinking Sanatogen, smoking dog-ends, and quoting Oscar Wilde, but it never amounted to anything. Faced with the Real Thing at parties, I fell instant prey to a diabolical tic, stone feet, and a falsetto giggle, and generally ended up by locking myself in the lavatory until all the girls had gone home.

Worst of all, I had no literary mentors to guide my pubescent steps. For years I'd lived on the literary roughage of Talbot Baines Reed and Frank Richards, but the time had now come to give up identifying myself with cheery, acne-ridden schoolboys. Similarly, the dream heroes of comic-books had to be jettisoned; I could no longer afford to toy with the fantasy of becoming Zonk, Scourge of Attila, or Captain Marvel, or the Boy Who Saved The School From Martians – girls weren't likely to be too impressed with the way I planned to relieve Constantinople, it had become increasingly clear to me that shouting 'SHAZAM!' was a dead loss, since it never turned *me* into a muscle-bound saviour who could fly at the speed of light, and as for the other thing, my school seemed to pose no immediate threat to Mars, all things considered. I needed instead, for the first time, a reality to build a dream on.

But I wasn't yet ready for adult ego-ideals. Not that I didn't try to find them in stories of Bulldog Drummond and the Saint (Bond being, in 1952, I suppose, some teenage constable yet to find his niche), but experience had already taught me the pointlessness of aiming my aspirations at these suave targets. Odds seemed against my appearance at a school dance, framed in the doorway, my massive bulk poised to spring, my steely eyes flashing blue fire, and my fists bunched like knotted ropes. Taking a quick inventory, I could tell I was short-stocked on the gear that makes women swoon and strong men step aside. And, uttering a visceral sigh (the first, as things turned out, of many), I sent my vast escapist, hero-infested library for pulping, and took up Literature, not for idols, but for sublimation.

The initial shock to my system resulting from this new leaf is something from which I never fully recovered. Literature turned out to be filled, yea, even to teem, with embittered, maladjusted, disorientated, ill-starred, misunderstood malcontents, forsaken souls playing brinkmanship with life, emaciated men with long herringbone overcoats and great, staring tubercular eyes, whose only answer to the challenge of existence was a cracked grin and a terrible Russian shudder. I learned, much later, that there was more to Literature than this, but the fault of over-specialisation wasn't entirely mine; my English master, overwhelmed to find a thirteen-year-old boy whose vision extended beyond conkers and Knickerbocker Glories, rallied to my cry for more stuff like Kafka, and led me into a world where bread fell always on the buttered side and death was the prize the good guys got. And, through all the borrowed paperbacks, one connecting thread ran – K., Raskolnikov, Mishkin, Faust, Werther, Ahab, Daedalus, Usher – these were all chaps like me; true, their acne was spiritual, their stammer rang with *weltschmerz*, but we were of one blood, they and I. How much closer was I, dancing sad, solitary steps in the Stygian garage, to the hunter of Moby Dick, than to Zonk, Scourge of Attila!

At first, I allowed the world which had driven me out of its charmed circles to see only the outward and visible signs of the subcutaneous rot. In the days following my acute disappointment at not being an insect, I wandered the neighbourhood dressed only in pyjamas, a shift made from brown paper, and an old overcoat of my father's, satisfactorily threadbare, and just far enough from the ground to reveal my bare shins and sockless climbing boots. By opening my eyes very wide, I managed to add a tasteful consumptiveness to my face, backed up by bouts of bravura coughing and spitting, and I achieved near-perfection with a mirthless chuckle all my own.

Suburban authority being what it is, I ran foul of the police within a couple of days, not, as I'd intended, for smoking reefers or burying axes in pensioners' heads to express the ultimate meaninglessness of anything but irrational action, but for being in need of care and protection. At least, this was how a Woolworth's assistant saw me. I had been shuffling up and down the aisles, coughing and grinning by turns, when a middle-aged woman took either pity or maliciousness on me, and tried to prise an address from the mirthlessly chuckling lips.

'What's your name?' she said.

'Call me Ishmael,' I replied, spitting fearlessly.

'Stop that at once, you horrid little specimen! Where do you live?'

'Live!' I cried. 'Ha!' I chuckled once or twice, rolled my eyes, hawked, spat, twitched, and went on: 'To live – what is that? What is Life? We all labour against our own cure, for death is the cure of all diseases ...'

I took a well-rehearsed stance, poised to belt out an abridged version of *La Dame Aux Camélias*, when the lady was reinforced by a policeman, into whose ear she poured a resumé of the proceedings to date.

'Alone, and plainly loitering,' said the copper. He dropped a large authoritarian hand on my shoulder. I was profoundly moved. I had been given the masonic handshake of the damned. Already with thee, in the penal settlement, old K.

'I shall go quietly,' I said, wheezing softly. 'I know there is no charge against me, but that is no matter. I must stand trial, be condemned, be fed into the insatiable belly of the law. That is the way it has to be.'

I gave him my address, but instead of leading me to the mouldering cellars of the local nick, he took me straight home. My parents, who hadn't yet seen me in The Little Deathwisher Construction Kit, reeled and blenched for long enough to convince the constable that the fault was none of theirs. My father, who believed deeply in discipline through applied psychology, gave me a workmanlike hiding, confiscated the existential wardrobe, and sent me to my room. By drawing the curtains, lighting a candle, releasing my white mice from bondage, and scattering mothballs around to give the place the camphorated flavour of a consumptive's deathbed, I managed to turn it into an acceptable condemned cell. Every evening after school (a perfectly acceptable dual existence this; the Jekyll-and-Hyde situation of schoolboy by day, and visionary nihilist by night appealed enormously to my bitter desire to dupe society) I wrote an *angstvoll* diary on fragments of brown paper torn from my erstwhile undershirt, and tapped morse messages on the wall (e.g. 'God is dead', 'Hell is other people', and so on) not, as members of the Koestler fan-club will be quick to recognise, in order to communicate, but merely to express. I got profound satisfaction from the meaninglessness of the answers which came back from the other half of our semi, the loud thumps of enraged respectability, unable to comprehend or articulate.

However, the self-imposed life of a part-time recluse was growing less and less satisfactory, since it wasn't taking me any nearer the existential nub which lay at the centre of my new idols. I was, worst of all, not experiencing any suffering, but merely the trappings. True, inability to cope with what the romantic novelists variously describe as stirring buds, tremulous awakenings, and so on, was what had initially nudged my new persona into life, but this paled beside the *weltschmerz* of the literary boys. Also, suburban London was not nineteenth century St. Petersburg or Prague, 1952 wasn't much of a year for revolution, whaling, or the collapse of civilisation, I was sick of faking T.B. and epilepsy, and emaciation seemed too high a price to pay for one's non-beliefs. Pain, to sum up, was in short supply.

It was *The Sorrows Of Young Werther* which pointed the way out of this slough of painlessness. Egged on by a near-delirious schoolmaster, I had had a shot at Goethe already, since a bit of *Sturm und Drang* sounded just what the doctor ordered, but I'd quickly rejected it. I wasn't able to manufacture the brand of jadedness which comes, apparently, after a lifetime's fruitless pursuit of knowledge, and the paraphernalia of pacts with the devil, *Walpurgisnacht-sträume*, time-travel, and the rest, were not really in my line. While I sympathised deeply with Faust himself, it was quite obvious that we were different types of bloke altogether. But Werther, that *meisterwerk* of moon-struck self-pity – he was me all over.

The instant I put down the book, I recognised that what up until then had been a rather primitive adolescent lust for the nubile young bride next door had really been 22-carat sublime devotion all along. It was the quintessence of unrequitable love, liberally laced with unquenchable anguish. Sporting a spotted bow, shiny shoes and a natty line in sighs, I slipped easily into the modified personality, hanging about in the communal driveway for the chance to bite my lip as the unattainable polished the doorknocker or cleaned out the drains. I abbreviated the mirthless chuckle to a silent sob, cut out the spitting altogether, and filled the once-tubercular eyes with pitiable longing.

The girl, who must have been about twenty-five, responded perfectly. She called me her little man, underlining her blindness to my infatuation with exquisite poignancy, and let me wipe the bird-lime off her window-sills and fetch the coal. What had once been K's cell, Raskolnikov's hovel, the *Pequod's* poop-deck, now took on the appearance of a beachcomber's strongbox. My room was littered with weeds from her garden, a couple of slats from the fence I'd helped her mend, half-a-dozen old lipstick cases, a balding powder-puff, three laddered stockings (all taken, at night, from her dustbin), a matted clot of hair I'd found in her sink, an old shoe, a toothless comb, and a pair of lensless sunglasses that had once rested on the beloved ears. Daily, I grew more inextricably involved. I began to demand more than silent service and unexpressed adulation. I dreamed of discovering that she no longer loved her husband, that she had responded to my meticulous weeding and devoted washing-up to the point of being unable to live without me. I saw us locked in each other's arms in a compartment on the *Brighton Belle*, setting out on a New Life Together.

In April I discovered she was pregnant. For one wild moment I toyed with the idea of claiming the child as my own, thus forcing a rift between her and her husband. But the plan had obvious drawbacks. The only real course of action was undoubtedly Werther's. Naturally, I'd contemplated suicide before, but an alternative had always come up, and, anyway, this was the first time that I had something worth dying elaborately for. I wrote innumerable last notes, debated the advantages of an upstairs window over the Piccadilly Line, and even wrote to B.S.A. to ask whether it was possible to kill a human being with one of their air-guns, and, if so, how.

In fact, if the cricket season hadn't started the same week, I might have done something foolish.

Death Duties

Up until now, it may not have been generally known that I live in a flat whose previous tenant shuffled off this mortal coil owing Selfridge's 12/6. But eighteen months is long enough to live with the increasing burden that this debt has come to represent; and since, on the question of responsibility, I am less of an island than most men you run across, I feel the need to spread the weight a little.

I know almost nothing about my predecessor, except that she departed this life peacefully at a commendably advanced age; I learned only a little more from the sad trickle of uninformed post that kept turning up after I moved in – she did the pools, she voted, she read The *Reader's Digest*, and she once spent a holiday in Torquay at a hotel that persists in inviting her to Gala Gourmet Week-ends which, from the manager's imploring circular, obviously won't be the same without her. At some time in her life, she purchased enough roofing-felt from a firm in Acton to warrant an annual calendar's gratitude, and, long before that, she had been a pupil at a girl's school in Roehampton which has now fallen on evil times and needs £5,000 to drive the woodworm from its ancient bones.

I dutifully sent these voices from the past back to the land of the living, marked 'Address Unknown', together with a brace of Christmas cards wishing her peace, a sentiment I feel bound to endorse. The only things I held on to (all right, this is probably a heinous crime under some subsection or other, but, believe me, I have pain in full for it) were a series of polite notes from Selfridge's, requesting the coughing-up of 12/6.

I had my own nefarious reasons for this peccadillo. Back in the early days, it came to me (not unlike a shaft of pure white light) that here I was with an invaluable index of consumer-tolerance, i.e., How far was Selfridge's prepared to go before they cried havoc and let loose the dogs of war? Were I ever to consider running up a fat bill with them, this information would stand me in the best of steads, since, the longer one can delay the payment of bills the better, inflation being what it is. (I have never been too certain what it is, actually, but as a kid I used to buy 1930 billion-mark German stamps at threepence a hundred, and a thing like that sticks in your memory.) Whatever Mrs. X. bought for 12/6 in 1962 doubtless goes out at around fifteen bob these days, and if she's reading this now under some Elysian hair-dryer, bless her, I hope she takes comfort from the thought that she got out while the going was good.

So, just to test the plan, I hung on, opening the three-monthly reminders, waiting for the sort of filthy innuendo *I* usually get in these circumstances about what a pity it is that I mislaid their bill and if I don't fork out in seven days, my humble and obedient servants will be round with the boys and have the telly back and no mistake. But nothing like that ever came. A year passed with the characteristic rapidity of its kind, leaves fell off the rubber-plant, the odd crow's foot stamped itself around my limpid eyes, and still Selfridge's continued to beg the pardon of the dead, and nothing more. I began to lay complex plans for capitalising on this inside knowledge. I walked the store, floor by floor, choosing one of them, two of those, fifty square yards of that, and so on, in order that when I came to make my move, I could draw up in an articulated truck by the goods entrance and be away from the place with a complete home in about ten minutes flat, with every chance of hanging on to luxury for a year or so. It was on one such drooling foray that my best-laid schemes ganged agley and withered on my brow in one fell metaphor; turning a sharp right at a bolt of Gustav Doré chintz, I came upon a scene that made the death of Little Nell look like a Groucho Marx routine; a tiny, lacey, delicate old lady, a butterfly emeritus exuding spiritual lavender, was pressing a small package on a salesman. She was going away, I heard her whisper, and she wanted to give him something to remember her by; he was, she said softly, not a salesman, but her dear, dear friend. I staggered out into, I believe, Gloucester Place, choking with Truth. She was, of course, *my* little old lady, or as near as made no odds; I'd become so enmeshed in the web of greedy intrigue currently on the loom that I had forgotten that there was more to my plan than just Selfridge's and I, two hard-boiled toughs who might one day face one another down at High Noon in Carey Street. Never for one moment had I paused to consider the old lady who had gone to join her ancestors with 12/6 worth of Selfridge's money. The one obvious reason why the store hadn't sent its bruisers round to collect the debt had up until then escaped me – that Mrs. X. had no doubt been a customer in those far-off Edwardian days when Harry Gordon Selfridge was still worrying about his mortgage repayments. Quite probably, she had been all set to go through the store for the last time, distributing cuff links and panatellas when the call for the long trip took her unawares, and it is more than clear to me that no one had informed Selfridge's of her passing. Suddenly, I saw her, a sweet soul, full of the simple goodness which is honed to a fine smooth finish on the *Reader's Digest* lathes; in my mind she sat filling in her Littlewood's coupons and praying for a first dividend to save the school from termites and provide everyone in Selfridge's with enough roofing-felt to last a lifetime. They must have missed her at the store, the living image of Whistler's mum, first up the escalator at the Sales ('Put them ornamented bathmats aside for Mrs. X., Esmond, she's one of our reg'lars'), smiling at Uncle Holly year in, year out, remembering every liftboy at Christmas ('It's little Horace, isn't it? My, we've grown, haven't we?'), a favourite with all the waitresses in the cafeteria, a paragon of virtue to the Accounts Dept.

I turned into Baker Street, the iron in my soul, another Raskolnikov with guilt for an old lady red on his hands. No doubt she had been missed at the store for eighteen months; rumours would be seething in the staff canteen, and, finally, half-apologetically, looking down into his tea-cup, someone would bring up the issue of her outstanding debt. At first, it would be excused, laughed off; but before long fifty years of graciousness would be swept away, and she would be written off as just another lousy customer, at one with the welshers and the shoplifters and the people who knocked things off shelves in the china department.

It was when I decided to make amends that the real horror of the things struck, in true Dostoievskian fashion; actions are irreversible, sin cannot be structurally altered. There was no way in which I could straighten the mess out; if I wrote to the store, explaining that their debtor was in no shape to square the account, they would wonder why I had taken nearly two years to contact them. It was even on the cards that I'd find myself opening the door to a couple of characters in fawn raincoats demanding to know what I'd done with the body. Similarly, were I able to trace her descendants, what could I say? ('Look, I hate to stir old memories, but your dear mother/aunt/sister owes Selfridge's 12/6'). How would they react to the stain imprinted by me on their loved one's reputation? I was the one who'd made her, post-mortally, a rotten financial risk, and dragged the good name of X through the mire. For all I knew, they might take it out on me by having me sent down for tampering with the mails, or something, and I understand they're handing out thirty years for that these days.

Last week, another demand-note turned up. The tone had shifted slightly to one of gentlemanly bewilderment; I knew the omens of old. I had to forestall the ultimatum; like Macbeth, I was in blood stepp'd in so far, that, should I wade no more, returning were as tedious as go o'er. Only one course of action lay open; I put a ten-bob note and a half-crown in an envelope, together with a note explaining that I had been laid up for two years with a wasting disease and only now was I beginning to pull through, and I hoped they would understand, theirs, with every apology, Mrs. X.

That ought to hold them for a bit. But you can never be sure about these things, and if they decide to have a whip round in the Soft Furnishings and send me a Get Well card and a jar of crystallised ginger, I may yet have to go on the run.

The Law of the Jungle
and Some of My
Other Headaches

'Sometimes,' said my wife, 'I wake up in the night and start thinking about the tigers down the road.'

That may not be exactly what she said, but it's as close a gist as makes no difference. I was singing the baritone part to the Wonderloaf commercial at the time, and at such moments I tend to become oblivious to surrounding activity. My wife, unfortunately, has no ear for music, else ours would be a joyful menage.

'If it's fresher than Wonderloaf, it's sti-i-i-ill in the oven,' I sang, not without charm.

'Elephants, too,' she said. 'I'm not sure it isn't more unsettling to have elephants.'

The commercial faded under pressure from Eamonn Andrews and a horde of his late-nite guests. Andrews sat in their boisterous midst, exuding that faintly sad embarrassment of his, looking rather like a bloke who'd turned up at the party without a bottle. It broke my heart, so I switched off.

'What was that about elephants?' I asked her.

'I said there were elephants down the road, and it bothered me. But it doesn't matter.'

'That's all right, then,' I said, with the limp air of a man fully aware that he has not put an end to a conversation.

She plucked a cigarette from her case, and I noted, with a thrill, the strength of my influence. It was perhaps the most tuneful cigarette on the box.

'Do you realise,' she said through the wreathing smoke, 'that at this very minute, animals from South American jungles are probably copulating in Regent's Park?'

For a girl without prejudice, she has a strange talent for pulling intolerant expressions out of nowhere.

'Maybe I ought to write to our beloved Marylebone M.P.,' I said. 'Or do you feel Mr. Hogg would consider it crass of me?'

'I don't know,' she said, her eyes full of bale, 'I have little first-hand knowledge of crassness. Only what I pick up here and there.'

'Are you calling my sensitivity to account?' I cried. It was, after all, Sunday night, and my articulacy had been honed to a fine edge on the *Observer* whetstone. Words line my throat in serried ranks, poised to spring.

She stubbed out her cigarette long before its appointed hour.

'I never thought we'd live near the London Zoo,' she muttered.

'You know what cunning swine these estate agents are,' I said. 'They concealed the fact that St. John's Wood represented Nature red in tooth and claw. Am I to blame?'

'It gets dark so early now,' she said. Her voice was ever soft, gentle and low, an ominous thing in woman. 'What if a tiger got loose?'

'They have no teeth,' I said. 'They're taken out under a local by-law. So you see . . . '

But she had gone.

It was clear that the Zoo had all the makings of a bone of contention. Only a tiny one, mind you. The sort that sticks in your throat and chokes you. I had enough experience to realise that if I was going to get any sleep that night, I'd have to work out a short, watertight argument for the preservation of Zoos, particularly those in Regent's Park. Now, were it possible to stand all the world's women in a straight line on an ascending scale of their affection for animals, you'd find Michaela Denis at one end and my wife at the other. All things considered, I'm really rather grateful for this; set Armand up with a lion in his lap and he's as happy as a sandboy, but I happen to be made of rather more urban stuff and tend to lean further towards the jug-of-wine-and-thou routine. Nevertheless, I'm prepared to live and let live, and I was convinced that with a few minutes of the sort of determination that comes with marriage, I'd be able to prove the indispensability of caged animals.

First of all, I had to establish that the bulk of humanity took a passionate interest in animals, and the best evidence for this is the fact that most newspapers have zoo correspondents on the books; of these, none is more eloquent than the *Evening Standard*'s Craven Hill, who, though he sounds like a station on the Bakerloo Line, writes with the deep feelings of a Noble Savage about his dumb friends. Take his November 6th column, for example, with its exultant headline: NEW MATE IS FOUND FOR THE SNOWY OWL, and read on:

' . . . a few years ago the zoo was fortunate enough to find itself with a useful breeding pair and from them several owlets were obtained. Then came tragedy. Last winter the female owl died, since when Zoo officials have been trying to find a possible second wife for the widower. Now it seems success may have been achieved. Inquiries at other menageries revealed that the Copenhagen Zoo had a mature snowy owl in residence and was ready to send its bird to Regent's Park . . . '

Clearly, the *Standard* believes (and it should know) that all London is agog for such news. There can't be too many of its readers who know what a snowy owl looks like, and I'll bet not more than a handful turned up at the funeral, but anyone's domestic heartaches make absorbing, emphatic reading, and surely the snowy owl implores the passing tribute of a by-line? After all, it takes the commuter out of himself, reminds him to count his blessings and that, but for the grace of God, he could be stuck in a cage with his sad memories, waiting for an unknown wife to be flown in from Copenhagen.

Time was running out, paced by my wife's bathwater, and so far all I had was a thesis and a newsclipping. But it was obvious that this human fascination for the animal predicament had a lot to do with the need for the London Zoo. A section of its large public must derive great consolation from being on the right side of the bars, and go home bloated with the relief at having been born a human being. Many of them, too, will have felt inexpensive pity for the first time in their lives, and that's always good for the soul. More philosophical visitors may even find huge satisfaction in recognising that all that evolution turned out to be worth while, since Man finally ended up with enough brains to stash animals away where they couldn't get at him. But that wasn't all. At this point, *Genesis I, xxvi* popped into my head, the way it will sometimes:

'And God said: Let us make man in our image, after our likeness; and let him have dominion over the fish of the sea, and over the fowl of the air, and over the cattle, and over all the earth, and over every creeping thing that creepeth upon the earth.'

It was abundantly clear to me that the London Zoo was the one place on earth where Darwin could have got together with the Pope and come to a working arrangement.

And another thing. To watch the metropolis's teeming millions (well, okay, maybe not *all* of them) on a visit to the Zoo is to become suddenly aware that no greater therapy exists for the pent-up neuroses nurtured in the concrete jungle. See the pretty people blowing raspberries at the camels, chucking peanuts at the monkeys, hammering on the glass walls of the snake houses, dropping pennies on the alligators, barking at the seals – exulting, in short, in their power over the impotent, crude beasts, and letting off the sort of steam you can't fire at neighbours, bosses, meter attendants, spouses, M.P.'s, and all those other molecules of society jostling for the chance of crushing you.

I padded into the bedroom on unhurried feet, leaned against the door-jamb with the calm nonchalance that marks the bearer of Truth, and said:

'The London Zoo lifts men's hearts, stimulates their minds, endorses their faith, releases their inhibitions, bolsters their confidence, and assuages their pain. It is an indispensable panacea. Is there anything else that could possibly do all those things?'

My wife yawned, and fear sank its teeth into my heart.

'There's whiskey,' she said, 'and it smells a lot nicer, too.'

Then she turned out the light.

Just a Gawp
at Twilight

There have got to be indoor equivalents to parks where elderly people can congregate, can stand and talk, or just gawp.
Conference report in **The Guardian.**

Take a good look at my passport photo. Me. Or as near as makes no difference, except, perhaps for any members of my wife's family who were looking for concrete proof to substantiate their convictions. Forget, for the moment, that it's apparently a picture of a man with two metal eyes and a glossy polythene skin. Forget that livid streak down his left cheek which he must have picked up in a thunderstorm. Forget even the plastic teeth clearly borrowed for the occasion. Look closely. See it? No, not the nobility; not even the glow of spiritual depth; but the vitality. With a dash of joy. Granted that the face seems to have been primed for the camera with a slug of Bile Beans and Vat 69, it is still the face of a man unable to conceal his profound zest for life.

You've probably guessed by now that the picture was taken when I was a mere lad; last September, in fact, in the closing stages of a *jeunesse dorée*, during which I deluded myself into believing that old age was something that happened to other people. Apart from a rather bleak pubescent period, when the sight of a dead worm or a melting ice-lolly hurled me into fits of Stygian gloom about Man's Brief Span On Earth, I'd never found it hard to persuade myself that at my birth the Great Foreman had turned His back for a second, and I had slipped through the factory before anyone had had time to build in my obsolescence. And I wasn't one of your compromise immortals, either, just a boxful of assorted dust and a Name to put on ashtrays every four hundred years or so; I was going to be there *in corpo* at Armageddon, waving the troops goodbye from the balcony.

I can't now pinpoint the day on which the fool in the photograph discovered that his paradise was established on a leasehold basis; it might have been the afternoon I took out an insurance policy to protect dependants I might have to leave behind; until then, not having any dependants, I don't suppose I ever faced the possibility of there being a behind to leave or that I was going to be the one to leave it. Or it might have been the day I rejected the idea of taking out a mortgage after the mental image it engendered of me finally celebrating the ownership of my home with a cup of gripe-water and a hobble round the garden on the arm of my favourite nurse. At all events, I spent last winter shrouded in a smell of camellias, peering at the stop press for the latest figures on lung-cancer and filling in the time between road-accident reports by scribbling wills on the backs of old envelopes. I gave our daily her cards after she heartlessly threw out my collection of fallen hair, and when I went down with flu my wife and I argued for three days about whether it was chic to be cremated, or merely exhibitionist.

However, I made it through the winter, and by the time the crocuses were shoving their heads up through the sod and shouting: 'LIVE! LIVE!' I'd got over the initial shock. All that remained of my romp through the Valley of the Shadow was a certain sadness about the eyes and a tendency to overdo the brave smile when someone asked me how I was. The real trouble is that, vulnerable as I now am, it doesn't take much to open up the old wound. In yesterday's *Guardian* there were two neighbouring stories, one instinct with pathos, the other luminous with joy. I'm referring, of course, to the report on boredom among the aged, quoted above, and the write-up of the Cameric Cigarette Card Club's annual outing from Croydon to Bristol. Now, I've always sneered at hobby fanatics, especially those who gather in excitable chattering groups to toast the latest matchbox, or huddle in mildewed cellars wet-nursing mush-rooms and crossbreeding mice. I do not believe the texture of civilisation to have been particularly enriched by models of Euston made out of hairpins, or the existence of dogs called Lord Jim Murchison III of Huddersfield who are incapable of doing anything but dribble on their rosettes. And I've always prided myself on a life too full to concentrate itself on the production of a giant marrow.

But that was in the old days, when I was immortal. Now I have to live with the knowledge that the time will come when my arthritic fingers will no longer be able to coax the magic cliché from its hiding-place on the keyboard, when all I shall be in a position to ask of life is that someone wheel me out into the autumn sunshine with my box of fading snapshots and a spittoon. *That's* when I'll regret my youth thrown away in idle hobbylessness.

'Members of the Cameric Cigarette Card Club travelled by coach from Croydon to Bristol during the weekend for their annual rally, because Bristol is still considered the home of the cigarette card . . . usually the club holds its meetings at Caxton Hall – "where we get mixed up with the weddings" – every three weeks.'

I can see myself reading such stories in the twilight of my days. Not for me the thrill of the summer dawn, the charabanc straining in the slips, the crates of Guinness lashed to the roofrack, the hordes of cheery cartophilists with their mouths full of ham sandwiches and their pockets bulging with swops, waiting to roar out of Croydon down the golden road to Bristol, to the home of the cigarette card, that western Mecca where men may sit and drink in the gloaming, remembering Flags Of All Nations, laughing over well-loved misprints, their fingers sticky with good old pre-war gum, and, here and there, a not-unhappy tear luminous beneath the rising moon. And then it's home to Caxton Hall to get mixed up with the weddings, corks popping, bouquets flying, rice pattering gaily on your bald head, pretty girls and laughing men. It's got the edge on monkey gland and Phyllosan any day of the week.

The closest I'll ever come to that will be a lucky gawp as the charabanc goes by. In fact, I suppose gawping *is* my hobby; at least, it's what I do when time hangs heavy. Go to the window and stare out. I live on the third floor, so there's often a nice topdeck-load of bus-passengers to gawp at. They gawp at me, too. Same when I'm in their position, going down Baker Street, gawping in at upstairs windows, at people in dentists' chairs, under dryers, secretaries taking dictation, men shaving, women knitting. Sometimes an empty room, with just a poodle gawping out. On the Tube, too. Gawp at shoes, behinds, other people's newspapers. Get gawped at all along the Central Line. And when I'm driving. At traffic lights, particularly. Gawp at man next to me, fishlike stares, no smiles, no contact. Gawpers lead lonely lives.

So any recommendation for meeting-places for elderly gawpers has my full support. A place to go once a week, a Caxton Hall for the underprivileged. I see myself, suddenly sprightly, with a straw hat at a racy angle, shouting a cheery farewell to my retainers: 'Just nipping down to the Assembly Rooms for a quick gawp, chaps. Don't wait up!' Trot down the road towards a warm glow in the sky, big hall full of the old familiar faces staring at me, and me staring back at them. Maybe we'll have visiting gawpers, or talent nights, with a dais, and an M.C., and even a little band. 'Good evening, good evening, good evening! Nice to see so many familiar eyes in the audience tonight, ha-ha-ha! And now, it's my pleasure and privilege to welcome our special guest, Mr. Leslie Polk, who's travelled all the way from Ilford to be with us tonight. Come on, Les, let's all have a look at you!'

By heavens, the more I think about it, the more I like it. In fact, I can hardly wait.

This Thing
with the Lions

The result of a bed-ridden afternoon, in which a romp through Hemingway concluded with a coda of Elsa the Lioness and the belief that enough was as good as a feast, however moveable.

The windbrake crackled in a gust of hot breeze. She looked up, but the leaves were still now. She could see the leaves through the open tentflap, and they were still. There was a lizard on the tentpole, near the top. It was the colour of old sand, and it had one yellow eye that did not blink. She whistled at it, twice; but it did not move. A muscle twitched in its shoulder, but it did not move. It is one of the brave ones, she thought. It is one of the few brave ones left.

The boy padded in with the drinks. Not that she drank so much any more, because drink did not do the thing that it used to do. All the drink in the world will not do that thing now, she thought.

'There are vultures,' said the boy.

'Yes,' she said. She watched the soda bubbles rise in the long glass, and burst, impotently. 'They have made a kill.'

'Yes,' he said. He looked away. 'Missy not go no more kill?'

'No,' she said. 'Not any more.'

'It is good,' he said. He pulled a tick from his black neck and snapped it with his thumbnail, carefully. 'It is not for lady, the thing with the guns.'

'That's right,' she said. She took the tall glass, and the ice bumped against her lips, and she thought: they will be cold now, the lips. But she did not laugh. 'No,' she replied, 'it is not for lady.'

Now in her mind she saw the wet platform of the Estacion Norte, and the great black tank engines, and the shuffling lines of khaki puppets and the anaesthetised faces of men who have lain beside the dead, and have got up and walked away. She saw the bars of the Madrid-Floride, and the Metropole, and the others, which were all the same after a while; like the fresh-faced boys who would never quite be fresh anymore. It was a long war, but they had still gone to it, and they had come back, more or less. Mostly less. She remembered the purple Spanish nights when she sat up in the room smelling of ordinario and cartridge-belts, holding their hands and telling them it did not matter the way everyone said it mattered, and that this thing with the woman was not all it was cracked up to be, anyway.

She could hear the bearers singing now, and she wondered about the kill. I hope they got a water-buff, she thought. I hope they got a big black sweating buck, one of those that keep on coming, even with a couple of 220 solid-grain Springfields buried in their guts; one of those big, hard males with the great spread of horn. Those were the best ones, in the old days. George would not let her go for them any more. Not after the time she had gone into the bush after the bull that had tossed him. She had dropped it, finally, with one so clean you had to part the forelock to find the hole. When she got back, George had been lying in the sun for three hours.

'*He was a tough one,*' she said.

'*I know,*' he said. '*I have lost a lot of blood.*'

'*Where did he get you?*' she said.

He took his hands away.

'*Oh.*'

'*That is the way it is, sometimes.*' He laughed, briefly.

'*Like Manolete,*' she said.

'*Yes.*' He began to cry. '*Like Manolete.*'

Things had been different between them after that, and he would not let her hunt the water-buffs any more. He did not like what it did to her, he said. So she sat around the camp, in the brass African heat, raising mongeese and cross-breeding scorpions. Sometimes she would stick pins in little clay models; but even that did not help.

She saw the first two boys come over the hill with the animal slung on poles between them. George walked alongside, carrying the big Remington by its strap. He waved at her, the way he always did, and she took another finger of scotch, and waved back. She got off the camp-bed and went towards them.

'It's a lioness,' she said, quietly. 'You son-of-a-bitch.'

'I didn't want to do it, but it happened that way. She came out of the bush, and no one had time to ask questions. She was a big one,' he said, 'and she was coming fast.'

She looked at the animal, with its guts torn open and its swollen teats hanging down, heavy with uselessness. She saw the belly full of old fertility, with the fat black flies buzzing around it.

'Cojones,' she said.

'I didn't want to do it,' said George again.

'I hate it when you kill females.' She looked at the bronze horizon. 'I hate it when you take it out on them.'

'Don't pity me,' he said, 'for Christ's sake.'

'She just calved. Is that why?'

'I didn't know she had cubs, I swear. When she came at us, I thought she was just one of the mean ones.'

'I hope it was a clean shot.'

He pumped a used shell out of the Remington.

'Some things you just don't lose.'

'You're so damned clever,' she said.

Two boys came up, grinning, with a basket between them.

'I brought you a present,' said George. He flipped open the lid. Inside there were three lion cubs; their eyes were still closed. There was something terrifying about their innocence.

'You and your goddamned metaphors,' she said.

He turned and walked into the tent. He pulled his bed a little further away from hers and sat down. He looked at the typewriter. Someday he would write about it, he thought. You can get rid of it when you write about it. He would write with symbols, so that when he was dead they would know he had been one of the big ones all the time. Turgenev was one of the big ones. And Flaubert. And Jack Dempsey. He was one of the big ones, too. And Ludwig van Beethoven. Turgenev and Flaubert and Dempsey and Beethoven and Peter Abelard and that old man in Key West who caught the biggest goddamned sailfish he'd ever seen in his life with a two-dollar rod. They were the great ones.

The next day he went up-country on a Government weevil survey. He did not get back for five months, and when he walked out of the bush, waving and calling the way he always did, it took six houseboys to get the lion off him.

'You didn't have to do that,' he said. He lay on his back in the tent, his one good eye bright among the bandages. 'You didn't have to alienate her.'

'I'm sorry,' she said. She smiled. She was looking better than she had for a long time. 'Elsa's funny with strangers. I had to send the other two away. I hope you don't mind?'

The eye glittered.

'As it turns out,' he said, 'you did the right thing.' He paused. 'How come you kept the third one?'

She did not answer. In the stillness, a baboon vomited. Elsa came in silently, lapped from a basin of pink gin, and padded out again.

'You got her pretty damned well trained.'

'We understand one another,' she said. 'That's all it takes. Understanding. And a little love.'

'That's fine,' he said. He tried to laugh, but the stitches dragged, and he fell back writhing. After a time, he said: 'You girls have to stick together. That's the way it is.'

'Yes,' she said, 'that's the way it is.'

That evening, they were closer than they had been since the time she worked the epidiascope at the Royal Geographic. They hand-wrestled, and laughed about the time he had smashed in the French ambassador's face with a bottle of Pernod on the train to Pamplona, and they went through the Book of Job together, looking for a title for that short story he planned to write some day; he felt good, with the old, half-familiar thing. At ten o'clock, he put his arm round her, and as he did, Elsa came in out of the dark and looked at him in a way that made him put his arm down again.

'What the hell,' he said. 'The stitches still hurt, anyway. I guess I'll just take a walk before we turn in.'

When he got back, the tent was dark. He sat down on his bed to take off his boots. There was a sudden roar of thunder in his ears, and a stench of stale caviare, and something heavy struck him in the back. He fell across his wife's bunk.

'What happened?' she said.

'There's something damned funny about my bed,' he said.

'*Whose* bed?'

He paused. 'You're not serious?'

'I took your mattress out into the open,' she said. 'It's a fine night. There are shooting stars. You'll be happier there.'

At three a.m., the monsoon broke. It was a good monsoon, as monsoons go, but the thunder was loud, and nobody heard the shouting. The boys found George three days later, after the flood went down. He was stuck in a gau-gau tree eight miles away. After four months, the hospital at Dar-es-Salaam sent him home.

'How was it?' she said.

'Fine,' he said. 'They said plenty of people go around with one lung.'

'It's good for a man to know suffering,' she said. A locust flew past, and she drew the Luger he always kept under his bed for medicinal purposes, and hit it three times. 'Animals suffer,' she said. 'The strong survive. That is the law. That is the only law that counts.'

He looked at her.

'I did a lot of thinking while I was in there,' he said. 'It isn't good for Elsa to be brought up with human beings. She is a lioness. She is being deprived of her natural inheritance.'

'I thought of that,' she said.

They had raw okapi meat for lunch, but he let Elsa have his share, because she was a year old now, and had a way of crunching bones that put him off his food. After the meal, Elsa and his wife sat around roaring at each other.

'I wish you'd teach me that,' he said.

'It'd only make Elsa more jealous,' she said.

He did not see much of them after that. They went out hunting at dawn, and did not return until sunset. Once, he wanted to go with them, but they would not let him take his rifle or his trousers, so he stayed behind and thought about the good time before the war and the time Dominguin got both ears and a tail and the time before that when he was a zoology student in Camden Town and he knocked a police-man's helmet off in Regent's Park Road. That was one story he had saved to write. He looked across the dung-coloured scrub to the dead tree where the vultures waited, cleaning their beaks. Somewhere it had gone wrong, he thought.

Something had come and it had waited a while, and then it had gone and it would not ever come back any more. And he was no nearer to knowing what it was than he had been on those pale mornings in Edgware in the days when his father had done that thing they did not talk about.

One evening, his wife came back alone. He saw her loping across the twilit scrub, growling. She stopped in front of him, and he saw the blood on her, and the bad marks, and the bald patch.

'It is over,' she said.

'Over?'

'She has found a mate.'

'That's how it is with kids,' he said. 'You bring them up, teach them everything you know, and they turn round and go off with the first creep who whistles at them.'

She laughed once, very high, and the vultures flew off in a rattle of black wings. She looked at him with eyes tinted yellow by the dying sun.

'Is that the way it is?' she said.

'Yes,' he said. 'That's the way it is.'

'I'm glad you told me,' she said.

Ugly to Look at
Disgusting to Know

Just in case you were lucky enough to have missed the following scrumptious gobbet of praline squeezed out by the sensitive fists of one Jean Campbell, let me stir your loins a little:

'A 61-year-old woman who was Gloria Swanson's contemporary has been wowing New York in the last week. All heads turn when she enters the 21 Restaurant. Her name? Dolores Del Rio. Dolores, who has been called the most beautiful woman in the world, is Mexican by birth. I have learned the secret of her lasting beauty that sometimes staggers men and women alike. For one day each week Dolores shuts herself up in a room with the curtains drawn. She lies on her bed, cream on her face, and her eyes covered with chilly lotion. Her telephone is never answered on this special day. She eats nothing but dietetic foods, speaks to nobody, and simply lies completely still, meditating.'

Does that slice of *Evening Standard* filet mignon remind you of anyone? If not, perhaps you haven't been around the Y-Pay-More Hotdog and Sauerkraut wagon currently pulling in the late-nite set at the corner of Praed Street and Edgware Road. Any evening this week, a 26-year-old man who was Ringo Starr's contemporary, but looks like Rudy Vallee's, has been wowing the glittering boulevardiers. All heads turn when he lurches out of The Rising Sun, his generous mouth encrusted with dried Guinness froth, stumbles nonchalantly across the road, and fetches up gasping against the steaming trolley. His name? Need you ask?

Alan, who has been called the ugliest man in the world, is British by birth. I have learned the secret of his lasting repulsiveness that sometimes staggers men and women alike, frequently at the same time, without using mirrors, and nothing up his sleeve. In fact, if at any time you come across a gang of citizens clearly staggering, in some otherwise sober corner of the metropolis, odds are that the nub of their disequilibrium is this very man. Since the question most often framed on the awestruck lip is: 'So young, yet so repugnant?' I think it only fair to let you in on the truth behind the legend.

For one day each week, Alan shuts himself up in a room with the curtains drawn. As this seems in other quarters to have had the effect of dressing mutton up to look like lamb, you are well within your rights in asking why, in his case, this has had the opposite effect. I am not qualified to speak of Miss Del Rio's motives in drawing the curtains and sliding the bolts, but my client pursues the same course for a number of specific reasons.

His chosen day, actually, is Saturday, it being the one day of the week in which he is at home, and his creditors are abroad, thus creating – in their minds, at least – a satisfactory, but wholly erroneous, solution to their collective problems. There was a time, of course, when a mere word down the telephone, the tiniest apologia on a snippet of scented notepaper, served to hold off the wolves. But this very soon gave way to his horizontal period, during which time it was his practice to peer from the window as the TV rental van, the butcher, the grocer, the bookmaker's aides-de-camp, the garage proprietor, the landlord, the newsagent, and all those other trusty craftsmen who give our cities their unique flavour of olde worlde greed and malevolence – to peer as these various predators turned up at his door, whereupon he would lie flat on the floor, out of sight, until the tumult and the shouting died and the swine departed whence they had come.

However, you must remember this, a kiss is still a kiss, a sigh is still a sigh, as time goes by, and it would be illogical of you not to admit that a debt is still a debt. Thus the closed-curtain routine, and the attempt to persuade all comers that the house has been struck by bereavement, bubonic plague, and so forth. Sharp at nine of a Saturday, just as a paternal hand at the B.B.C. is dropping the needle on *Teddy Bears' Picnic*, Alan's creditors fall in in close order, and take it in turn to scream obscenities and amounts through the letter-box, while our hero lies on the bed in the darkness, his face screwed up, and an evil-smelling cork from a flagon of cheap burgundy stuffed in each ear. This probably accounts for the fact that while Miss Del Rio has ears like tiny white conches, and a skin smooth as watered silk, Mr. Coren's homely countenance is as lined as those of the old lady whose job it is to pose in the Andes for the Photographers of the Year, and his ears have made strong men weep and bishops turn aside.

Like Miss Del Rio, he too can be found at such times with cream on his face, and while the imagination can only boggle fitfully at what exotic preparation soaks rejuvenatingly into her lily-like complexion, no such mystery surrounds my subject. His comes out of an aerosol bottle, with the object of softening up his bristles for the keen swift blade, but since he buys his blades in packets of five on a Monday, by Saturday the packet is empty, a fact never discovered until after the aerosol has turned to alabaster on his chin. As the blades come in a handy dispenser-cum-disposal unit, the only course open to him is to fish around in the thing with a bent paper clip, until an old rusty blade drops out, covered in those tell-tale black marks which testify to its having been used for sharpening his wife's eyebrow pencil. Due to all this, the primary result of his application of facial cream is a network of spidery wrinkles around the eyes, and a hysterical laugh that has confounded psychiatrists the world over.

Not to be outdone by any actress old enough to be his grandmother, Mr. Coren, too, has chilly lotion on his eyes. It is a rare compound of Vat 69 and aerated water kept in large quantities beside his bed to help him through this day of fasting and meditation. Since both the curtains and his nerves are tightly drawn, the operation by which the elixir is carried to his supine lips is successful only very rarely, with the result that his eyes come in for constant bathing at 70 per cent proof. Whether for his reason, or others, these eyes are small, yellow, and webbed with hideous red veins, rather in the manner of addled sparrows' eggs.

On his special day, he too never answers the telephone, partly because no news is good news (in his case, it has never been otherwise), and partly because the telephone company is loth to reconnect him to any of their exchanges, for reasons which are intriguing, but infortunately *sub judice*.

On the Del Rio question of dietetic food he is, of course, adamant. Over-eating is to him a shameful and disfiguring vice, and he prefers to subsist mainly on stuffed olives, twists of lemon peel (ideal for those schoolgirl hands for which he lives in hope), Twiglets, and the nourishing morsels of cheese-and-pineapple which are given away in our generous hostelries, in return for no more than the odd firkin or two of life-giving liquid yeast. Because of this punishing regimen, he has managed to contain his huge bulk within a small area, just south of his belt.

All that remains to be described is that process of meditation to which he owes those ravages which are no concern of Time's, but are merely the by-product of the age in which he was raised. Sometimes, he just lets his mind wander freely over the Inland Revenue, his editor, lung cancer, Overkill, road accidents, or how much Strontium-90 is in the hops this year; but sometimes he is more specific, and attempts to understand the Trade Gap, or Cost Curves, or the Balance of Payments system, and on one notable occasion he tried gamely, having promised it to himself for years, to compare and contrast Niki and Nedi, the M.L.F. and the A.N.F., Nato and Seato, Efta and Gatt, the Six and the Seven, and other figures of contemporary mythology. When his wife finally returned from her mother's, she asked the bald, muttering ancient at the door for information as to her husband's whereabouts, and he broke down and cried like a baby.

But worst of all, since life imitates advertising, there are occasions when he passes a fresh-faced, lithe, and laughing man on the Harrods escalator, who waves at him and promises to meet him in the coffee-shop at 11.30. 'Who was that?' asks Mrs. Coren. 'That's Jon Rayman,' mutters her husband, 'we were at Oxford together.' 'Really?' cries the spouse, 'he looks *years* younger!'

On his special day, in the darkness, he thinks about that most of all.

Learn Omniscience the
Easy Way Today!

Purnell's New English Encyclopaedia *comes to you every week as an absorbing and lavishly illustrated magazine. But this is a magazine of permanent value. Week by week it grows into a valuable library of learning. From A to Z week by week. In just 18 weeks you will have in a permanent binding Volume I of the complete 12-volume set. The next 18 weeks will see the completion of Volume II . . . and so on, until you have all 12 volumes.*

Advertisement

You may not have known me in the old days before Sir Mortimer Wheeler and Sir Bernard Lovell and the rest of the editorial gang at Purnell's got their hands on me, because I didn't get around very much. How could I? A shy, diffident lad with less General Knowledge at his fingertips than you could shake a stick at, I spent most of my time listening to lectures at Caxton Hall trying to cure my stammer, my unsightly blushes, and a curious, self-effacing, pigeon-toed walk that is the legacy of something now lost forever in the prenatal mists. I was, you see, the victim of a specialist education (O, where were the Snows of yesteryear?), the War, and a highly individual brand of galloping acne, all of which left me in post-adolescence as one of those flowers born to stammer unseen, and rightly so. I became the sort of chap who turns up at beer-and-cheese parties carrying a bottle of Veuve-Clicquot to apologise for the pointlessness of his presence, and spends the rest of the evening standing

184

in the corridor with a sickly grin on his face hanging up the coats of new arrivals, and occasionally slipping off to the bathroom to twist alone. (Thinks: *Imagine what a twit I must have seemed before receiving the first instalment of* Purnell's New English Encyclopaedia! *I can laugh now, but it wasn't funny at the time, I can tell you! Then, one day, when I was trying to think of why the chicken crossed the road, to the embarrassment of all, my best friend leaned across and whispered: 'Stupidity!' in my ear. And then I knew what I had to do.*)

It's all so different now. It seems like only yesterday that the first instalment of Purnell's arrived through my letter box. It *was* only yesterday, actually. (Thinks: *Time was, I wouldn't dare make a joke like that! What confidence knowledge gives you! Just wait until I get the 'Wetnurse – Wit' instalment in October 1968, packed with new jokes for all the family!*) There it lay, No. 1, 'A – Aconite', and today I'm a changed man. I spent all day reading it up and committing it to memory and in the evening my wife gave a small dinner party, as a sort of, well, launching ceremony. Nobody special, just a few of her friends who have come, over the years, to regard me as a blot on the history of the human race.

It wasn't without a certain trepidation that I awaited the first arrivals. After all, general knowledge may give you that extra something, but I wasn't sure I could confine the conversation within the – let's face it, Sir Mortimer – rather narrow limits of A – Aconite. At 8.30, the Plunketts arrived, and I leapt to greet them with such eagerness that something which I can only describe as fear flashed across George's eyes as he drew my arms from his neck.

'Hallo, old man,' he said. 'My, but you're lucky to see us! Nearly had a nasty accident coming off the old A3, didn't we, Phoebe?'

'Accident?' I cried. 'Not one of the 350,000 that occur each year in Britain?'

'Probably one of those,' said his wife, a curiously wry lady.

'It has been estimated,' I said, leaning nonchalantly against the door-jamb and folding my arms, 'that if traffic continues to increase at the present rate, and accidents commensurately, 10,000 people will be killed annually in Britain by 1980.'

185

The Plunketts looked at me with new interest.

'What about a drink?' said George, and I smiled at him confidently.

'Experts,' I said, examining a fingernail, 'believe the greatest amount of alcohol a driver should have in his blood is 0.1 per cent. In practical terms, this means a limit of $1\frac{1}{2}$ pints of beer, or three small tots of spirits.'

'I'll have three small tots of spirits, then,' said Phoebe, and we all laughed uproariously, though I couldn't see why. Roll on May 1966 when the 'Jerboa – Jutland' instalment will tell me all I need to know about Jokes.

Soon after this, the Hubbards and the Folletts arrived together, and before long we were all sitting round talking about Abidjan, the capital of the Ivory Coast which has a population of nearly 200,000, many of whom live in Treichville, an industrial suburb. Later, pleasantly exhausted by our chatter (would you believe it, *nobody* had heard of Abbas the Great, the most important sovereign of the Persian dynasty of the Safawids [1557–1628]? Harry Hubbard had heard of somebody called Baldwin, but I think he was just making the name up to show off. Anyway, I pretty soon changed the subject to acanthocephala – a class of parasitic worms, not unlike tapeworms – and that shut him up, I can tell you!).

At dinner, I was a little chastened to discover that my wife had been unable to obtain aardvark steaks at Sainsbury's, but I got over the lull in conversation by describing, in what must have been fascinating detail, the running of an abattoir, and how infected carcases and entrails are rendered down for fertilizer and soap. At the end of the main course, I turned to my wife, a smile playing somewhat mischievously about my lips, and said:

'Would you like me to accumulate the plates, dearest?'

She was oddly silent, but nodded briefly.

'Yes,' I continued, standing up, 'let me be the accumulator, ha-ha-ha. Not, of course, the apparatus able to absorb energy and give it back when required . . .'

'No?' asked Alfred Follett, his face rapt.

'No,' I replied. I laughed. 'I shouldn't like to be coated with lead dioxide (or PbO_2) which is then transformed into lead sulphate (or $PbSO_4$), you know. It would undoubtedly kill me.'

I caught a wistful look in Alfred Follett's eyes, and I realised that he would probably have given anything to know as much as I do about accumulators. But it isn't given to all men, that kind of knowledge; one has to know how to use it wisely.

After dinner, the talk ranged over every conceivable subject, from abyssal deposits to abu-Nuwas (an eighth century Arab poet who ridiculed the life of the desert), from William Aberhart (the famous Canadian politician) to the accordian. I cannot remember ever having had so sophisticated an evening. The time seemed to fly by on Achilles heels, I think is the expression. It felt like no more than an hour after dinner when everyone got up to leave; it was in fact one hour and eleven minutes, although my wife said that the time was so packed with interest and information and so on, that it felt like four, which cheered me up enormously, since I had been afraid that the guests might have felt cheated by my not being able to tell them any more about Aconcagua than the fact that its chief industry is rearing sheep and goats.

The Plunkets and Folletts had already run down the path by the time I'd helped Winnie Hubbard into her coat, so she and Harry were the only ones I could ask to come again.

'Sorry, old chap,' said Harry, 'but we're off to Greece for a month tomorrow.'

'Really?' I said. 'Not to Achaea, by any chance, that district in the north of the Pelopennese which is 1,160 square miles in area, with a population of 236,000?'

'No,' he said. 'To Athens.'

Athens! By heavens, so near and yet so far! Next week's instalment, in fact.

'You *must* come and see us when you get back,' I said.

I hope they do. I can't wait to hear what I have to say about it.

ALAN COREN

THE SANITY INSPECTOR

Alan Coren is 'dreadfully witty . . . arguably the
funniest writer in Britain today'
THE SUNDAY TIMES

Alan Coren was out when the Sanity Inspector came
round. Which may be why this outrageous collection
of simply improbable anecdotes and wild flights of
fantasy was ever allowed to reach the public.
The author modestly claims to be merely a symptom
of our society. If he is, fact isn't only stranger than
fiction, it's a lot funnier too. So look out for salmon
fishing ferrets, Emma Bovary in support tights,
Pope Lew Grade, man-eating earwigs and a
travelling hairdresser with one leg and a parrot on
his shoulder.
And look out, because when the Sanity Inspector
calls on you, *you* might actually be there.

'He is one of the funniest writers I have ever read
from any country'
ESQUIRE

CORONET BOOKS

ALAN COREN

GOLFING FOR CATS

From the 'dreadfully witty'* author of the bestselling
THE SANITY INSPECTOR, contributor to *Punch*
and chronicler of the doings of Idi Amin, here is
another sparkling collection of brain-tickling humour.

'He is one of the funniest writers I have ever read
from any country'
ESQUIRE

'There is no man quite like him when it comes to the
business of wringing laughter from the reluctant
lips of those who read the printed word'
EVENING STANDARD

'Probably the most infallibly funny columnist now
writing'
BBC WEEKLY WORLD

'Coren never needs to manhandle his images with
muscular twists to make them fit their satirical
purposes. They simply slot into place, neat as a
knife between the ribs'
IRISH TIMES

*The Sunday Times

CORONET BOOKS

DIRK GIRLING ETC

WOULD YOU BELIEVE THIS TOO?

n December 1963 a Florida police patrol picked up a chimpanzee for speeding. It was a hoax, however: a hidden carnival showman was working the pedals; the chimp was only steering.

A Suffolk dairy collected 1,800 empty milk bottles from the home of a single elderly woman.

A leading cabaret attraction in San Francisco is 'a topless grandmother of eight'.

Captive squids suffering from depression commit suicide by eating their own tentacles.

CORONET BOOKS

ed. WILLIAM DAVIS

THE PUNCH BOOK OF HEALTH

Hallo. Undress please, will you? Don't argue, there are other patients waiting.

Right. Take this book and at the first sign of depression read one article, with Scotch or brandy. Repeat every five or ten minutes until symptoms subside. It won't cure coughs, lumbago, gout or arachnophobia, but it will make you feel better about whatever you think is wrong with you. And yes: this is one medicine you can safely keep within reach of children.

Ingredients: articles by Richard Gordon, Basil Boothroyd, Keith Waterhouse, Alan Coren, Brian Inglis, Miles Kington, Vincent Mulchrone, Clove Barnes and others. Plus cartoons by Graham, ffolkes, Heath, Larry, Roth, Langdon and others.

CORONET BOOKS

ALSO AVAILABLE IN CORONET